THEMES
for early years

MINIBEASTS

AVRIL HARPLEY & ANN ROBERTS

THEMES
for early years

Authors Avril Harpley and Ann Roberts
Editor Jane Bishop
Assistant editors Sally Gray and Libby Russell
Series designer Lynne Joesbury
Designer Rachel Warner
Illustrations Chantal Kees
Cover Lynne Joesbury
Action Rhymes, Poems and Stories compiled by Jackie Andrews
Songs compiled by Peter Morrell
Assemblies chapter by Lesley Prior

Designed using Aldus Pagemaker
Processed by Scholastic Ltd, Leamington Spa

Published by Scholastic Ltd, Villiers House, Clarendon Avenue, Leamington Spa, Warwickshire CV32 5PR

© 1997 Scholastic Ltd   Text © 1997
5 6 7 8 9   0 1 2 3 4 5 6

The publishers gratefully acknowledge permission to reproduce the following copyright material:
Addison Wesley Longman Ltd for the use of 'Who's That In Beetle's House?' which appeared in playscript form in *English Through Topics: Minibeasts 2* © 1993, Sue Palmer (1993, Oliver & Boyd). **Jill Atkins** for 'The Earthworm' © 1997, Jill Atkins, previously unpublished. **Clive Barnwell** for 'Five Little Ants' © 1997, Clive Barnwell, previously unpublished. **Ann Bryant** for 'Caterpillar Munch' and 'The Boogie Bugs' © 1997, Ann Bryant, previously unpublished. **Sue Cowling** for 'Bellyfoot' and 'How To Make A Butterfly' © 1997, Sue Cowling, previously unpublished. **Sadie Fields Productions Ltd** for the use of *The Happy Tree* by Joy Cockle © 1996, Joy Cockle (1996, Tango Books an imprint of Sadie Fields Productions Ltd). **Jean Gilbert** for 'Worm' and 'Fly' © 1997, Jean Gilbert, previously unpublished. **Hazel Hobbs** for 'Spiders' © 1997, Hazel Hobbs, previously unpublished. **Jack In A Box** for the use of 'A Famous Spider' by Jackie Andrews © 1997, Jackie Andrews, previously unpublished. **Jean Kenward** for 'Snail' © 1997, Jean Kenward, previously unpublished. **Karen King** for 'Speedy' © 1997, Karen King, previously unpublished. **Elizabeth Matterson** for help in trying to trace the authors of 'This is Little Timothy Snail' and 'Under A Stone...' from *This Little Puffin* compiled by Elizabeth Matterson © 1969, original source unknown. **Trevor Millum** for the words to 'Tongue Twister' © 1997, Trevor Millum, previously unpublished. **Tony Mitton** for 'Ladybird, Ladybird', 'Little Caterpillar', 'The Ant's Tea Party', 'The Spider's Tea', 'Minibeast Moods' and 'Miniature World' © 1997, Tony Mitton, previously unpublished. **Judith Nicholls** for 'Lady Dot!', 'Spidery-Spy' and 'There's A Spider In My Bath!' © 1997, Judith Nicholls, previously unpublished. **Sue Nicholls** for 'Red and Black', 'The Centipede' and 'Snail's Pace' © 1997, Sue Nicholls, previously unpublished. **Gill Parker** for the music to 'Tongue Twister' © 1997, Gill Parker, previously unpublished. **Jan Pollard** for 'Little Spider' © 1997, Jan Pollard, previously unpublished. **Lesley Prior** for three assemblies © 1997, Lesley Prior, previously unpublished. **John Walsh** for 'Join The Queue' (a shape poem) © 1997, John Walsh, previously unpublished. **Maureen Warner** for 'Chrysalis' © 1997, Maureen Warner, previously unpublished. **The Watts Publishing Group** for *Creepy Crawly Caterpillar* by Kara May © 1994, Kara May (1994, Orchard Books Ltd).
Every effort has been made to trace copyright holders and the publishers apologise for any inadvertent omissions.
British Library Cataloguing-in-Publication Data A catalogue record for this book is available from the British Library.

ISBN 0-590-53685-0

The right of Avril Harpley and Ann Roberts to be identified as the Authors of this work has been asserted by them in accordance with the Copyright, Designs and Patents Act 1988.

All rights reserved. This book is sold subject to the condition that it shall not, by way of trade or otherwise, be lent, hired out or otherwise circulated without the publisher's prior consent in any form of binding or cover other than that in which it is published and without a similar condition, including this condition, being imposed upon the subsequent purchaser.

No part of this publication may be reproduced, stored in a retrieval system, or transmitted, in any form or by any means, electronic, mechanical, photocopying, recording or otherwise, without the prior permission of the publisher. This book remains copyright, although permission is granted to copy pages where indicated, for classroom distribution and use only in the school which has purchased the book, or by the teacher who has purchased this book and in accordance with the CLA licensing agreement. Photocopying permission is given for purchasers only and not from borrowers of books from any lending service.

CONTENTS

INTRODUCTION

The theme of minibeasts can be used to help young children broaden their knowledge and understanding of the world. A world where every little thing can still have a useful function.

Children will learn that certain insects have an important role to play in the world, that they can be useful to us and that we shouldn't be frightened of them. Some minibeasts look alien and frightening whilst others are quite beautiful and children also need to be able to recognise those which can be dangerous.

The theme of minibeasts covers insects and other small creatures. It will give a fascinating view of a form of life which is able to change shape or can adapt to live in quite different environments, eat different foods and move in different ways.

INVESTIGATION

Throughout the year certain minibeasts will be very much in evidence and available to you, so the children's interest will be heightened. Take advantage of any unpredictable happenings such as a sudden influx of ladybirds or butterflies which can prove an exciting experience for the children and a valuable source of learning.

Minibeasts provide an ideal opportunity for first hand investigation as they are easily accessible and can be found where children live and play, making them available whether you live in the town or the country. Whilst the children work they will be involved in the skills of investigation, observation, classifying and recording.

This book aims to provide a flexible approach within a framework for adults who work with children, it provides a starting point and stimulus for exploring and investigating the natural world.

CURRICULUM LINKS

The ideas in this book provide lively, practical and workable activities which are suitable for use by adults working with children of varying abilities and levels of maturity between the ages of three and six years old. All the activities, while firmly rooted in structured play, are designed to prepare children for the National Curriculum and Scottish 5–14 Guidelines. The ideas also fit well into the six Areas of Learning for under-fives recommended by the School Curriculum and Assessment Authority in the document *Nursery Education: Desirable Outcomes for Children's Learning on entering compulsory education.*

The book is divided up into six main activity chapters with one each on ladybirds, snails, worms, spiders and butterflies and one looking at all kinds of insects.

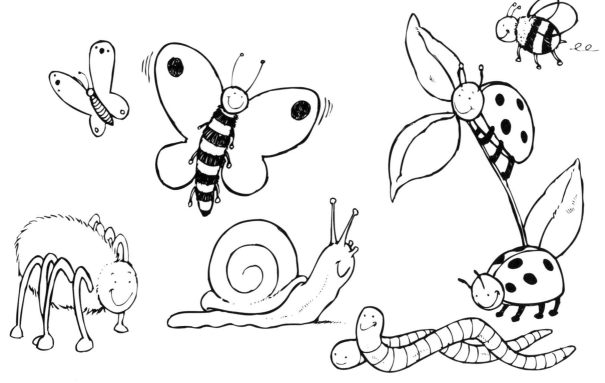

HOW TO USE THIS BOOK

Themes for early years – Minibeasts is one of a series of books which have been written for adults who work with young children at home, in playgroups, in nurseries and in reception classes.

The activities offer ideas grouped under a common theme and act as a stimulus to investigate a particular minibeast. Some of the activities are science based whilst others approach minibeasts from stories, poems and the imagination. The length of time spent on each activity may vary with the season, the local environment, the availability of resources and the interest of the children.

The first five chapters are each based on a specific minibeast and the sixth is based on a variety of different ones.

TOPIC WEB

The topic web on pages 8–9 is designed to aid planning by showing how each activity relates to the National Curriculum and Scottish 5–14 Guidelines. To ensure that children receive a broad and balanced curriculum, the activities in each chapter have been selected to cover all the subjects of the curriculum. Although each activity targets a main curriculum area many also have cross-curricular links.

ACTIVITY PAGES

For each activity a learning objective is identified which shows the main subject area and explains the purpose of the activity. A suggestion is given for the appropriate group size, but individual circumstances may influence your choice of the number of children in the group. Working with smaller groups, for example, generates better discussion opportunities and allows the quieter children a chance to contribute.

A list of materials and equipment needed before the activity can begin is provided and any preparatory work necessary such as making or setting out equipment is listed.

Step-by-step instructions are outlined on how to carry out each activity and although explicit instructions are given, most of the activities can be adapted for different ability levels. The main points to bring out in discussion are provided, and finally follow-up activities are suggested which either extend the given activity or provide some new approaches to try.

DISPLAY

Ideas for how to set up displays based on the Minibeasts theme are provided giving clear instructions of materials needed, how to set up the display and ways of using it to involve the children. Always allocate plenty of time for the children to examine the displays individually and organise a group discussion time to talk about what they have seen and learned.

ASSEMBLIES

The chapter provides ideas for planning assemblies or group sharing times related to the theme. Each assembly has its own practical ideas on how the children can be encouraged to contribute, to reflect on the specific theme and a relevant prayer and song are also suggested.

RESOURCES

A useful selection of songs, stories and poems on the minibeasts theme are given in this section. Much of the material has been specially commissioned to complement this book. All of the resources are photocopiable.

PHOTOCOPIABLE SHEETS

Eight photocopiable sheets, each linking with an earlier activity in the book, are provided. Make sure the children know what they have to do and that any new vocabulary is understood beforehand. Allow time afterwards to discuss the sheets with the children in order to ascertain how much they have understood.

RECOMMENDED MATERIALS

Details of information books, stories, songs and poems linked to this topic are listed on the final page as a useful resource.

THEMES
for early years

EXPRESSIVE ARTS

Planning towards the National Curriculum and the Scottish National guidelines 5-14

PHOTOCOPIABLE

PREPARING FOR PRIMARY SCHOOL

Children in the early years learn through first hand experiences, notably through play. They need to have opportunities to try out different skills and to learn concepts as they approach the requirements of the National Curriculum.

The National Curriculum was established to standardise the subjects, and the subject content, taught at all levels of a child's education. The intention is that any child will be able to go to school anywhere in the country and find the same areas of the curriculum being covered. These subjects are: English, Mathematics, Science, History, Geography, Design and Technology, Information Technology, PE, Art, Music and RE.

The activities suggested in this book cover all areas of the curriculum. Many are directed at small groups working together, but could equally be used with pairs of children or for children working alone. All children learn at different rates and have different paces of development so will need to be viewed by you, very much as individuals.

TOWARDS LEVEL ONE

The National Curriculum programmes of study apply to children who have reached the age of five. They were written to suit the abilities of children who have reached their fifth birthday and have spent anything from a term to a year (depending on the part of the country in which they live) in a reception class. The National Curriculum provides an overall programme of study for each subject and requires teachers to assess the level of attainment of each child at the end of the Key Stage. The assessment is carried out partly through nationwide testing, but for the most part, it is left to the teacher's professional judgement to allocate an overall level to each child.

Before this time, children will be working towards its requirements under the provisions of the School Curriculum and Assessment Authority's Desirable Outcomes. The skills they will need include communication, observation, social and physical skills. These are not acquired through chance but through the provision of a carefully planned selection of activities. The ideas in this book allow for these vital skills to be developed through first hand experiences.

THE SCOTTISH GUIDELINES 5–14

In Scotland there are National Guidelines for schools on what should be taught to children between the ages of five and fourteen. These are divided into six main areas: English Language, Mathematics, Environmental Studies, Expressive Arts, Religious and Moral Education and lastly Personal and Social Development. Within these main areas, further subjects are found, for example within Expressive Arts there is art and design, drama, music and PE.

Most nurseries will find that the experiences they are offering children will provide a good foundation for this curriculum. The activities in this book have been specially written to prepare for many aspects of it, and will also fit well into the pre-five guidelines issued by the local authorities throughout Scotland.

The activities centred around the themes are shown in separate areas of the curriculum on the topic web (pages 8–9) to help with planning. The children's personal and social development is an ongoing theme and is incorporated throughout the activities outlined in this book.

CHAPTER 1
LADYBIRDS

This chapter includes using a ladybird number line, examining live ladybirds at close-hand and even writing an advertisement for a new house for a homeless ladybird!

LADYBIRD LINE

Objective

Mathematics – To recognise and use numbers up to ten.

Group size

Small group.

What you need

Picture books or wrapping paper showing ladybirds and leaves for reference, real leaves, adhesive, scissors, felt-tipped pens, pencils, white / red paper, black dots, green sugar paper.

Preparation

Show the children the actual leaves and the pictures in the books which you have collected. Cut ten large leaves from the green sugar paper, and attach them to the wall in a long line at the children's height.

What to do

Ask the children to make some ladybirds by drawing simple shapes either on white paper and colouring them in or using red paper and then cutting them out. Alternatively, you could cut these from the wrapping paper depending on the time available and the abilities of the children.

Working in sequence from left to right place ladybirds on the leaves which are fixed to the wall. On leaf number one place one ladybird, on leaf two, two ladybirds and so on.

Extend this basic idea if the children are ready to develop it further, by fixing only one ladybird on to each numbered leaf then sticking the corresponding number of black dots onto each ladybird in turn.

Once the whole number line has been completed let the children check that everything is correct by matching numbers to the ladybirds or the dots. Use the number line throughout any future maths activities on your topic, and integrate it into a display of the ladybird work (see page 62).

Discussion

How many spots do ladybirds have? A ladybird has two wings, if you put one spot on one and two on the other how many would there be? Refer to the number line whenever an opportunity arises to count on or count back using the numbers to ten.

Follow-up activities

✧ Use photocopiable sheet 88 and play the number game. This is a mini version of the group number line and requires the children to use a dice to complete the dots.
✧ Play dominoes.
✧ Use a ladybird shape with detachable spots on to denote how many children may play at the sand tray or sit at the craft table, for example.

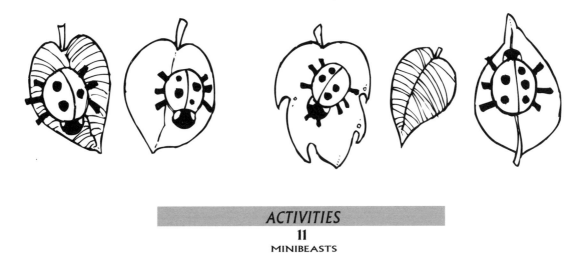

MINI MESSAGES

Objective

English – To develop story writing skills and learn about the conventions of a book.

Group size

Six to eight children.

What you need

Sheets of A4 paper, pencils, colours, scissors, adhesive. Collect some used postcards, notes, envelopes, labels, signs, tickets, lists, till receipts to show ways of sending messages and information.

Preparation

Use a sheet of A4 paper to prepare a sample book following the illustration here. Write messages to cut out and slot into the cut marks. Use interactive messages such as an invitation to a picnic, with a reply slip depending on your storyline.

What to do

Explain to the children that they are going to produce a story book and that their books will contain removable paper messages that are essential to the story. Show them the book you have prepared already and the sample message items you have collected.

Give each child a piece of paper and show them how to fold it into a book. Some children may need help cutting the tramlines. Identify the front and back covers and see if the children can work out which pages will be for the words and which pages will be for the pictures.

If the children need help to start their story, provide a starting point such as: 'A ladybird saw a ....' then stop. Ask the children to close their eyes and imagine what the ladybird saw. Link this to things the children already know about ladybirds – where they live, what they eat, their different colours and spot-markings.

Encourage the children to think about the variety of types of messages they could use and show them your sample book again.

Depending on their ability and emergent writing skills, let the children continue on their own or let an adult write down their ideas for them to illustrate.

Encourage the children to finish by producing their own book covers.

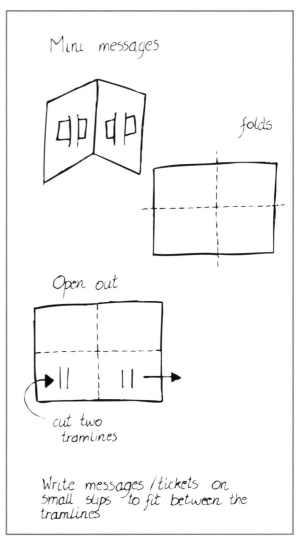

Discussion

Talk about the sorts of books they have seen. Ask what is on the front and back covers. Where will they find the author's name, the publisher, the price? Ask the children: Who would read the book? What will be written on the messages? Why have you put in this message?

Follow-up activities

✧ Make miniature versions of these books by using half the A4 paper.
✧ Make ladybird-shaped books and books with pop-ups.
✧ Have a post-box for the children to send messages to each other.

HOW DO YOU FEEL?

Objective

RE – To explore feelings and behaviour.

Group size

Up to ten children.

What you need

The story of *The Bad-Tempered Ladybird* by Eric Carle (Picture Puffin), two sheets A2 paper, a sheet of A4 paper for each child, pencils, scissors, adhesive, colouring materials.

Preparation

Collect photographs from magazines of people's faces showing different emotions, such as happy and sad expressions. Ask the children to sort and classify these. Talk to the children about what makes them feel happy or sad. Label one A2 sheet of paper 'I feel happy' and the other 'I feel sad' and record the children's comments as they speak.

What to do

Read to the children the story of *The Bad-Tempered Ladybird*. It tells of two very different ladybirds who meet over a breakfast of aphids. One is a bully and wants all the aphids, the other one stands up to him and suggests sharing them. The bad-tempered ladybird eventually backs down with the comment 'You're not big enough for me to fight.'

Give each child a sheet of A4 paper, folded in half and opened out again. On one side let the children illustrate what makes them feel bad-tempered and on the other side show the consequences of negative feelings. This might include arguing over which programmes to watch on TV and then the TV being turned off so they miss everything, or wanting to play with someone who always grabs the best toy for themselves.

Discussion

Ask the children, when do you feel bad, what do you do, what do you say? Why did the bad-tempered ladybird say the friendly one was not big enough to fight? What did the friendly ladybird say? Why do you think he was bad-tempered? What would you say? What would you do? Discuss how we don't like feeling angry, bored or sad and that we do like feeling happy. Encourage the children to tell you when someone has done a kind action and celebrate it together.

Follow-up activities

✧ Use puppets to explore different types of behaviour in stories, such as The Wolf in 'Red Riding Hood' or The Ugly Sisters in 'Cinderella'.
✧ Look at pictures in some magazines to show how people's faces change with their feelings. Let the children try to show different emotions on their faces and then ask the other children to guess which emotion is being shown.
✧ Make up a story about the ladybird who was different (some are yellow with black spots).

LADYBIRD LAND

Objective

Design and Technology – To design and construct a ladybird hand puppet.

Group size

A group of two or four children.

What you need

Two pairs of black gloves, black and red pompoms (from a craft shop), piece of black felt, adhesive, Velcro, black pipe-cleaners, pictures of ladybirds or real ladybirds to observe for details, green fabric/felt, leaves.

Preparation

Look at and discuss the pictures/real ladybirds together, giving the children the chance to observe shape, size and other details. Gather the craft materials and make a rough drawing of a ladybird and draw or list the resources they might need.

What to do

Explain to the children that they are going to make ladybirds and that the gloves are going to provide the 'environment' or background for the ladybirds.

Use the pompoms as the ladybird bodies, cutting a black pompom in half and sticking it to a red to produce the basic body shape. Cut spots out from the felt, and stick onto the main body. Use pipe-cleaners to make the legs for the ladybirds, and join these to the body with adhesive. You may need to hold each leg so they bond sufficiently.

Whilst the ladybirds are drying, concentrate

on the background or environment. Use the real leaves as templates to cut out leaf shapes from the green fabric. Attach the fabric leaves to the gloves using Velcro. Attach small squares of Velcro to the ladybirds and they too can be placed on the gloves. The ladybirds can 'fly' from leaf to leaf.

The children can wear a glove as a puppet which will also provide a background 'scene' for the ladybirds which can be detached and moved around the glove to tell a story.

Discussion

What colours are on a ladybird? Where do they live? Where could you find them? How do ladybirds move? What could we use to make the spots on the ladybird? (Look at the materials and colours and discuss.) How many spots will you have? How many leaves do you want to put on your glove, so that the ladybird can move and change?

Follow-up activities

✧ Act out the action rhyme 'Ladybird, ladybird, fly away home' using the gloves to tell the rhyme.
✧ Make some aphids which ladybirds like to eat to put on the leaves. Cut up a green pipe-cleaner into small pieces and glue these onto the leaves.

WATCH THIS SPOT

Objective

Mathematics — To recognise pattern, size and conservation of number.

Group size

Pairs, or small groups up to four.

What you need

A collection of simple templates of ladybirds which vary in size, and amount of spots on each ladybird – with a maximum of six spots, a dice with up to six spots on, adhesive and a large piece of card on which the ladybirds will all fit. Collect some real leaves or make some paper leaves with thin, green paper.

Preparation

Stick the ladybirds onto the card base, with some space between them. Cut out some paper leaves from green paper, if necessary.

What to do

Gather the group or pair of children that are to play the game and tell the children they need to be looking very carefully at the size of the ladybirds and the number of spots on their bodies.

Begin by focusing on one ladybird and counting the spots on the whole of its back. Then count each wing individually. Use this as an opportunity to extend to addition if possible.

Now ask the children to throw one dice and look for a ladybird with the same amount of spots on its back. When they count and match the number they can lay a leaf over that ladybird.

Continue the game until all the ladybirds are covered. The one who has covered the most ladybirds is the winner.

Discussion

Pointing to some specific ladybirds ask how many spots there are. If you add the spots from both sides of the ladybirds wings how many do they make? Are any of the ladybirds the same? Which is the ladybird with the most spots? Which of the ladybirds has the least spots?

Follow-up activities

✧ Use the ladybird templates to do some oral addition after the game. Use the templates for some practical subtraction – count all the spots then hide some away and ask for a count up of those remaining.
✧ Make a collection of objects with spots on – attempt to count the spots, this may need adult participation and support.
✧ Print using objects that make 'spots' such as cotton reels or buttons; count as you print.

MUSICAL LEAVES

Objective

PE / Drama – To develop gross motor skills such as running, dodging, flight and landing.

Group size

Up to 15 children (depending on available space).

What you need

Chalk or coloured tape, black sugar paper or card, music such as Tchaikovsky's 'Sugar-Plum Fairy' (music with distinct movement sounds).

knees bent. Do this several times so that you can observe how individual children manage the task.

Next introduce the idea of stopping when the music stops. Play the music and when it stops tell the children they have to find a leaf to stand on. Practise this a few times and establish rules such as being completely inside the leaf shape.

To extend the game, place a different number of dots on each leaf and tell the children that this time the amounts of dots determine the number of children allowed on each leaf. (Ensure you have correctly counted the children and dot ratio!) Following this, start to reduce the dots to eliminate some children. These children must sit down near the adult and help to observe that the remaining children are playing fairly until the end of the game.

Preparation

Use chalk or tape to mark out leaf shapes on the ground (a hall or outside on a playground), large enough for the children to stand on and well spaced out. Cut out large black dots (about the size of a plate) and place these on the leaves using the tape double-sided to hold them in place. The children should be comfortably dressed or change into loose clothing so that they can move freely, wear plimsolls or have bare feet.

What to do

Ask the children to each stand in a space but not on the leaves. Talk to them about how ladybirds move, fly, land. Practise crawling and flying (running and lifting off the ground) and landing safely with

Discussion

How do ladybirds fly? In the game when are you allowed to 'fly'? When you land, what do you need to think about so you do not hurt yourself? Do all ladybirds fly? What happens if you are not right inside the leaf?

Follow-up activities

✧ Make a small-world replica of this game and let a child control putting the music on and off.
✧ Use the music as a background and change the imaginative play area into a garden with large leaves, pretend grass and ladybird scull caps (available in educational catalogues) so that the children can role-play being in the world of a ladybird.

LOOKING FOR LADYBIRDS

Objective

Science — To explore and investigate ladybirds in their environment and to observe them for a short term indoors.

Group size

Four to six children.

What you need

Access to the outdoors with plants and bushes, pictures of ladybirds (or make one with red and black paper), scissors, marker pen. For each child a kit consisting of: a hand lens, a piece of white sheeting, a pooter: a jar with a lid, two wide bendy straws (one marked red, one marked green), Blu-Tack, tape, a piece of muslin.

Preparation

Display pictures of ladybirds or make your own giant-sized ladybird labelled to clearly show the wings, head, body, legs and colour. Make the pooter: tape muslin over the end of the red straw to stop ladybirds from getting into the mouth. Make two holes in the jar lid and push the straws through. Hold in place with Blu-Tack. Demonstrate how to use the pooter. Place the green straw near to the insect and suck on the red straw. The ladybird will be vacuumed up into the jar. Make sure the children suck up with the right straw.

What to do

The best time to find ladybirds is in late summer. Explain to the children that you are going outside to find out where ladybirds live. Show the children the pictures and discuss what you will be looking for outside.

Impress on the children that ladybirds are living things and should not be harmed. Lay the sheeting underneath a bush and gently shake the bush. The insects will fall onto your sheet; there may be a variety of insects on the sheet. Supervise the children while they use the pooters to carefully collect some ladybirds. Collect some leaves from the plant as well.

Let the children bring the ladybirds in the jars and the leaves back indoors for close observation. They can watch how each ladybird moves on different surfaces, look at the shape of its wings, its head and body. Count the legs, see where the eyes are placed. Experiment to see if it likes water and what it likes to eat — try leaves from different plants and small pieces of fruit and vegetables.

Draw a map or a picture showing where the ladybird was found. What were the conditions — was it a dry / damp / dark / sunny / shady place? After observing the ladybirds carefully return them to their habitat.

Discussion

Ask: Where should we look for ladybirds? (They like to feed on aphids so look on plants and rose bushes.) How can you tell it is a ladybird? (Look for its flying wings and distinctive colouring.) Why do you think it is so brightly coloured? (The colour is a warning to its predators that it tastes nasty.) There are 42 different known types of ladybirds in Britain, all with different numbers of spots. Some ladybirds are yellow and black, some are black with red spots.

How can we pick it up without hurting it? How can we carry it? How will we keep the ladybird in our room? What will it need?

Follow-up activities

✧ Transfer the information onto a simple computer database program to store and retrieve later.
✧ Provide red and black spotted capes for role-play.

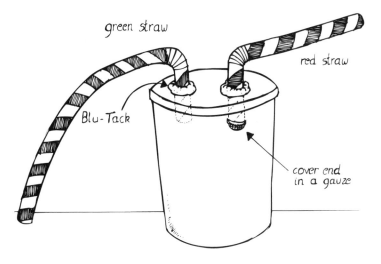

green straw

red straw

Blu-Tack

cover end in a gauze

HOME WANTED!

Objective

English – To encourage descriptive writing for an audience.

Group size

Eight to ten children.

What you need

Pictures and advertisements of houses for sale, reference books about ladybirds, paper, pencils, a computer if available, the poem 'Ladybird, ladybird' from page 71.

Preparation

The children should be aware of the sort of environment a ladybird needs for survival. In summer they need greenfly to eat, these can be found on rose bushes, and they need room to fly. They will lay their eggs between April and July. In winter ladybirds need somewhere to hibernate – like cracks in paths, in and under tree bark. Let the children use and explore the reference books.

What to do

Say the poem and explain that after harvest time farmers used to set fire to their fields to cleanse them, destroying the ladybirds' homes. Look at the examples of advertisements of houses for sale. Discuss the sort of things they describe – number of bedrooms, kitchen, bathroom, garden.

Imagine that the ladybird has lost her (or his) home. What sort of a new home will she look for? Encourage the children to think about the needs of a ladybird such as protection, food source,

environment. Bearing these needs in mind ask the children to make up an advert describing a home for a ladybird.

The children can write their adverts or an adult can help by scribing them or keying them in on a computer and printing them out.

Discussion

What are the dangers for a ladybird? Why do they need food close by? (They cannot see very well, they sense by touch.) What sort of food do they need? Why would a tree or shrub want ladybirds living on them? (Because they eat greenflies.) How does a ladybird fly? (The wings are hidden underneath the brightly coloured wing cases.) What would the world look like to a minibeast? (Plants would be huge. A child's hand would be the size of a giant.)

Follow-up activities

✧ Make a large tree/shrub out of paper and card, and place model ladybirds on it.
✧ Construct a home for a ladybird using boxes and scrap material. Think of all the things it might need for winter hibernation.
✧ Look at the similarities and differences of a minibeast home and the children's own homes.
✧ Make a passport type book for a ladybird.
✧ Make up a group story about how the shrubs and flowers were unhappy because the ladybirds have gone.

CHAPTER 2
SNAILS

Investigate spiral snail shapes in mathematics and music, make clay models in art, and learn to coil and crawl like snails in PE, in this chapter.

SHAPE AND SIZE

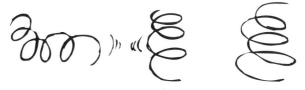

Objective

Mathematics – To describe and discuss shapes and patterns.

Group size

Small group up to six children.

What you need

Collections of spiral shapes, springs, snail shells, pictures showing spirals, contrasting pictures and objects of circle shapes and spheres, baskets and containers for sorting.

Preparation

Throughly wash any empty snail shells.

What to do

Let the children fully explore the objects and talk about the pictures tracing around the shapes with their fingers.

Ask them to start by sorting the items into two groups – circles and spirals. Next take the group of spirals and sort them into more precise sets. Let the children choose the criteria for sorting such as small, pointed spirals, wide bands or by colour.

Discussion

Look at the different spirals and compare the widths and heights – some are flat and wide, others thin and tapering, conical, winding. Does the spiral always twist one way – to the left or the right? Why

do you think there are bands of pattern on the shell? (Each band is a year in the life of the snail. As the snail grows the shell gets larger at the entrance.) The shell can be sealed for protection against predators or if the weather gets too hot or cold. Can the children think of other creatures that live inside shells? (Tortoises, turtles, shellfish.) Are these the same shape as snails shells?

Follow-up activities

✧ Cut spiral shapes out of paper circles. Colour and draw patterns on the paper and then hold it in one hand and cut into the shape. Keep cutting and following the edge of the circle, turning the paper as you go until you come to the centre.
✧ Try finger knitting or French knitting making long wool shapes that can be sewn into coils and spirals. Use ribbon braid stuck onto card to create differently sized spiral shapes.
✧ Find curling shapes in the environment: fossil spirals, the leaves of plants, water going down the plug hole.
✧ Look for curling shapes on our own bodies – ears, hair curls. Make fingerprints with black ink and compare the whorls, loops and shapes.

SNAIL SONG

Objective

English – To focus on sound patterns in letters.

Group size

Up to six children.

What you need

Paper, pencil, coloured pencils, card, felt-tipped pens, a hand mirror, scissors, Velcro, words starting with 'sn'.

Preparation

Write the word 'snail' and a selection of other words containing the pattern 'sn' onto pieces of card with the felt-tipped pen and cut into strips.

What to do

Sort out three of the word cards and show and tell them to the group. Let the children say the words and examine how their tongues feel in their mouths when they say the 'sn' sound. Let them look in the mirror to see the position of their tongues in their mouths.

Shuffle the 'sn' words then place them face up on the table to make silly sentences such as: sleepy snails snore; snooping snakes sneeze; slow snails snacking. Do this as a group then let the children work in pairs, one writing the sentence and the other one illustrating. Come back together as a group and share the sentences.

Choose some of the children's favourite sentences and develop a rhythm with the words to make a song, perhaps to the tune of a favourite nursery rhyme. Draw a large snail shape and Velcro the words around it to form a useful word bank.

Discussion

Can you think of some more words that start with this sound? Does anyone's name have the 'sn' sound? Was it easy to draw the pictures? Were there any funny pictures that made them laugh? Which did they prefer doing: writing the sentence or drawing the picture?

Follow-up activities

✧ Collect words beginning with these letters – S N A I L. Use these words to make up a sentence about snails such as: Snails Never Attack Iced Ladybirds.
✧ Write the words in a snail shaped spiral

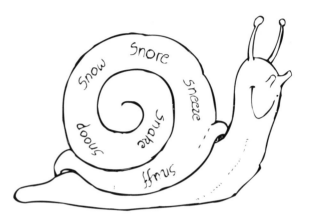

✧ Make a disc game using the prefix 'sn' and suitable endings, ow, ap, ake, ail. Use a large picture of a snail with a window cut out to show the word endings written on the circle underneath. Turn the snail shell to reveal the new words.

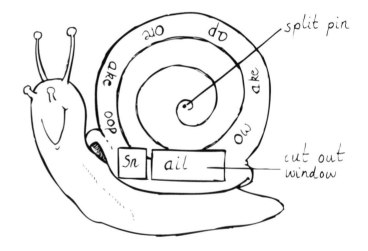

> **SN word bank**
> snake, snaky, snaking, snore, snoring, snoop, snoopy, snooping, sneak, sneaky, sneaking, sneeze, sneezy, sneezing, snarl, snarling, snatch, snatching, sniff, sniffing, snort, snorting, snout, snuffle, snuffling, snack, snacking.

SNAIL TRAIL

• •

Objective

Science – To explore how a snail moves and feeds.

Group size

Pairs and small groups.

What you need

Snails, a sheet of stiff clear transparent plastic, a large jar with damp green leaves, a saucer of milk, a saucer of water, a hand lens, A4 sheet of paper.

Preparation

Collect some snails in the jar with the damp leaves. Put the snail onto the plastic.

What to do

Hold up the plastic so that the children can observe the snail moving. The whole body section is called the foot. Watch the muscles ripple as it moves along. The trail of slime helps the snail to move over rough surfaces. Notice how it is able to stick upside down on the plastic sheet. Put a drop of milk onto the plastic and watch the snail lick it up.

Some children may like to handle the snails. Encourage the children to look closely at the snail using a hand lens. Put out the saucers of milk and the water and watch which they go to. Most snails eat plants but some eat other small creatures.

Carefully return the snail to its environment. The children should wash their hands.

Discussion

How do you think the snails are able to crawl up the sides of the jar or hang upside down on the plastic? What do they feel like when they move on your hand? Do you think they will stick to any kind of material? How could we find out? How could you find out how fast it can move? How do you think it moves?

Follow-up activities

✧ Use the activity 'Twist and turn' (page 27) to make snail trails.
✧ Make trails in shaving foam or a prepared cornflour and water mix.
✧ Make snail shapes in cooking by coiling dough and pastry, and winding cooked spaghetti.

ROUND AND ROUND

. . . .

Objective

Art – To use clay to develop the skills of rolling, joining to make spirals and using clay tools.

Group size

Small groups of four to six depending upon resources and space available.

What you need

Clay (self-drying if you do not have access to a kiln), clay tools, string, clay work boards or hessian, rolling pins, clay crafting tools, washable aprons, saucers (to make a circle shape), string, clay slurry which acts like glue for joining, a jam jar with water and bits of clay in.

Preparation

Prepare the clay by cutting it into lumps and kneading all the air out. Knead the clay until it is fairly soft. The children need to see how this is done and they can then do it for themselves. If the clay is slightly hard put some water onto it and then work it, if it is getting too dry then put damp paper towels over it to retain the correct consistency. Cover the table and ask the children to roll their sleeves up and put aprons on. Make sure there are adequate tools for the group.

What to do

Give each child some of the clay and ask them to roll it out using the rolling pins and the baseboards or hessian to avoid the clay sticking to the surface. Using a saucer as a template cut round it to make a circle of clay. Keep the bits of clay to one side.

Take a piece of string and practise making spirals. Using the oddments of clay press the string in coils onto the clay and lift it, it should leave a clearer imprint on the clay. Now place the string in a large spiral that covers the saucer shape. This is the snail's shell. To make the body of the snail roll out a sausage-shape piece of clay, making it flat and twisting it slightly round to make the body shape to fit around the shell shape. Join the body and shell with the clay slurry that has been prepared in the jam jar and hold for a few minutes to allow joining to take place.

Make the snail's antennae by rolling clay into two little pieces and joining them to the head, marking the eyes and mouth by using the clay tools which you have available.

Once the snail has been made then leave it to air-dry or take it to the kiln when it has sufficiently dried out. The snail can be painted or glazed depending on the type of clay you have used.

Discussion

What other spirals do you see? (Spirals such as a corkscrew, helter skelter, plants such as ivy that have spirals to grip to walls, shells.) What marks do the different tools make? What are the different parts of the snail? What do you use to join pieces of clay together?

Follow-up activities

✧ Collect objects that are spiral shaped.
✧ Use string and paints to make spiral shapes on paper or card.
✧ Make spirals with icing bags and icing on greaseproof paper.
✧ Make biscuits/cakes that are spiral shapes – making the mixture up and rolling and twisting it into spirals then cooking it.
✧ Collect various empty shells, looking for the spiral pattern, tracing it with your finger then copying the basic spiral shape using a pencil to record it.

MR SNAIL MOVES SLOWLY

Objective

Music – To investigate pace and speed in music, concentrating on opposites (fast and slow).

Group size

Small groups of four or six.

What you need

A large music stave, pictures of snails, elephants, panthers, bees, Blu-Tack, the story of 'The Hare and the Tortoise', a collection of instruments including tambourines, drums, shakers, instruments that can be used for fast and slow sounds.

Preparation

Pin up or draw a large music stave on an easel or a whiteboard, so that the group can see it clearly. Tell the children the story about the hare and the tortoise. (One day a hare and tortoise meet and they agree on a race, the hare is certain he will win, because he can run faster, he is so sure of himself he stops and falls asleep, meanwhile the tortoise slowly keeps going and in the end beats him.) Discuss fast and slow animals and minibeasts. Look at the pictures collected and lay out the instruments.

What to do

Talk about the music stave, explain that it is a place where we can write down music. Point to the bottom line and explain this is where we can write low sounds and the top line is for high sounds. Demonstrate a deep note and then a high note to make sure the children understand the difference.

Talk about 'fast' and 'slow' and demonstrate by clapping your hands quickly then slowly. Take the example of an elephant that is heavy and moves slowly and therefore would be represented by a low sound. Choose a drum or tap on your legs to represent a suitable sound. Place a picture of an elephant on the music stave to help the children realise that when they see this they make the corresponding sound. Add two or three more pictures of the elephant to correspond to the number of beats you want the children to make.

Now introduce fast sounds using a picture of a hare, bee or panther as an example and a shaker to represent a quick sound when shaken at speed.

Once the children can understand 'fast' and 'slow', mix up the pictures and put a new sequence onto the stave. Ask the children to make the appropriate series of sounds to represent the musical story.

After several sessions extend this by introducing low and slow, fast and high together. Emphasise that not all high notes are fast, and not all low notes are slow. This activity is an early introduction to reading music and later children will use notes instead of pictures.

Discussion

What animals / minibeasts move slowly? (Snails, elephants, worms, caterpillars.) What animals / minibeasts move quickly? (Panthers, ants, bees, butterflies.) Can you make a fast and slow sound using the same instruments? What instrument would you use to represent the hare / tortoise and why? Can you make a fast / slow sound using your hands / feet?

Follow-up activities

✧ Use photocopiable page 89 to sort animals into fast and slow groups. Let the children colour the groups of animals in different colours or cut them out and group them on paper. Able children may also be able to write 'fast' and 'slow' under the relevant pictures.
✧ Collect fast and slow objects such as cars, balls, clockwork toys.
✧ Make some simple percussion instruments of your own (yoghurt pot shakers for example) and make some group music!

CURLING AND COILING

Objective

PE – To develop and perform movements and patterns.

Group size

Up to 12 children in a line (larger group will need more than one line).

What you need

A large free space, the finger poem 'This is little Timothy Snail' page 68.

Preparation

Teach the children the poem 'Timothy Snail'. The children should be comfortably dressed or change into loose clothing so that they can move freely, wear plimsolls or have bare feet.

What to do

Ask the children to think about the way in which a snail moves. Let the children find a space and begin the session with slow, controlled stretching and curling up movements. Start with the body curled over and with the head on knees, arms extended forward. Gently raise the trunk and at the same time lift the hands up the body and past the ears. Finish by extending the arm stretch upwards, stretching as they wave their arms and wiggle their fingers. Pretend these are the snail's feelers. Relax slowly returning to the starting position. Repeat this movement.

Now stand up and tell all the children to hold hands in a long line. The leader of the line dances freely in the space with the line following. The leader then begins to dance in decreasing circles until she can no longer turn around and the line has formed a spiral shape behind her. At this point the last child in the line turns and becomes the leader unwinding the circle and dancing freely around the room.

Repeat the movement pattern with the new leader. Finally let the children find a space and sit down. Say the finger poem together and encourage the children to join in.

Discussion

What did you think about the coiling dance? Did you like it? Did you feel lost? If yes, when? Have you got any ideas for a snail game?

Follow-up activities

✧ Play other ring games such as 'Round and round the village' and 'London Bridge is falling down'.
✧ Teach gentle forward rolls: have a gym mat for the children to work on. Teach them how to place their hands and feet close together on the floor then look through their hands, curl up and softly roll over.
✧ Draw a collection of things that move slowly.

CATCH THE SNAIL

Objective

Geography – To use prepositional language and geographical language in early route making.

Group size

A group of four to six children.

What you need

A large sheet of card (60cm × 60cm), felt-tipped pens, crayons, a story that contains a route such as *Hansel and Gretel, Goldilocks and the Three Bears* (both Traditional) or *Rosie's Walk* by Pat Hutchins (Picture Puffin), pictures of snails, cardboard, Sellotape, A4 paper.

Preparation

Place the card onto a large table or space on the floor, have drawing materials ready for use.

What to do

Read some of the books to the children to establish the idea of making a journey.

Next, use the large sheet of card to show a bird's eye view of an area, showing landmarks such as a lake (circle of blue), a forest (a collection of trees), a start and finish, a mountain/hill (series of rocks). Either draw the baseboard yourself or ask the children to draw the features for the map. Remind them that a snail is very small so a little bush may seem like a forest and a puddle like a lake!

Make some counters to use by drawing a snail, then folding a square piece of card and using Sellotape to stick it onto the picture so that it will stand upright.

Once the baseboard is ready, invite the group to talk about the various features and introduce prepositional language such as – around, through, above, below.

Ask the children to move their snail counter along a route telling their own snail story. Make sure the rest of the group listen so that they avoid repeating what has gone before. Once they have all told their story of a route ask them to draw it in sequence like a cartoon as a reference.

Discussion

Which way are you going next? How do you get over the wall/hill? What features are on the map? Which is the easiest way to go? Which is the hardest thing on the map for the snail to pass?

Follow-up activities

✧ Make a large-scale 3D map using a board/cloth as a base and placing objects on it to represent a lake (bowl of water), or a mountain, piles of rocks (boulders), a forest (plants). Draw a 2D version to represent it, to develop early map-making skills.
✧ Make a model of a street using boxes.
✧ Make a fold-out book in which you could write a sequential story that has a beginning, middle and end, like a journey.

SEEING LIKE A SNAIL

Objective

Religous/Moral Education – To show sensitivity and consideration towards each other and other living things.

Group size

A small group of four children.

What you need

Brown card, elastic, a detailed picture of a snail's face, adhesive, scissors, greaseproof paper.

Preparation

Tell the children about snails and their lack of eyesight. Explain that the snail is not completely blind, it can see light and dark, but cannot make out the shapes of things.

What to do

Study the picture you have of a snail's face and try to look for the eyes. Hold up the greaseproof paper and try to see through it. Discuss what it is like not to be able to see clearly and how difficult it could be. Be very sensitive to any children in your group who have impaired sight and may be very self-conscious about wearing spectacles.

Cut out a circular shape of brown card for each child, to represent the snail's face, use a hole puncher to make a hole on either side of the mask. Tie on the elastic to fit each child's head. Take the mask off and cut out eyes, next cut out circles of greaseproof paper and glue over the eye area.

Make sure the children are in a safe area where they cannot walk into anything harmful. Let them put their masks on and carefully try to move around. Once they have experienced this take off the greaseproof paper and let them try the same process. Notice together how much easier it is when we can clearly see where we want to go.

Discussion

How does it feel when you look through the greaseproof paper eyes? Is it easy to move? What do you remember when you cannot see well? If you sit and shut your eyes what can you hear? When you are moving do you listen more carefully? Talk about people who have sight problems. How can we help them? (By gently holding and guiding them, describing things to them.) Do you know any other creatures who find it hard to see? (Worms, badgers.) How should we behave if we meet someone who is blind? (Give them more time and space, and tell them about what you can see and notice.)

Follow-up activities

✧ Play Blind man's buff in a safe area.
✧ Play Kim's game – cover up a tray of objects and try to memorise them.
✧ Make the home corner into an optician's and try on some sunglasses or play spectacles.

CHAPTER 3
WORMS

Set up a wormery to observe real worms burrowing, recreate a worm's environment in the sand tray, make worm sock puppets and slither and slide in PE in this chapter.

TWIST AND TURN

Objective

Art – To make contact prints to represent worms burrowing underground.

Group size

Four to six children.

What you need

Paper, brown paint, plastic trays, aprons, scissors, pictures of worms or real worms, paintbrushes.

Preparation

Cover the table if necessary, cut the paper to the size of the plastic tray, then trim slightly. Mix up the paint (the children can help if you wish), put it in the paint trays and spread it out lightly. Put aprons on the children. Display pictures and books, collect real worms to observe.

What to do

Study the pictures or observe the real worms. Allow children to touch the real worms if they want to (don't force unwilling children to try this!) but make sure they wash their hands well immediately afterwards. Notice how the worm is quite a uniform shape but gets thinner at the tip of each end.

Encourage the children to use their index fingers to dip into the paint and to make 'worm' shapes in it. When they have created a suitable pattern, carefully lay the paper on top and press gently. Peel off the paper to reveal the print of the worm and their burrows. Ask the children to make different-sized worms and in different burrows.

After the activity is completed and the paint is dry, count how many worms you can see on their pictures.

Some children may not enjoy touching real worms or the sensation of touching paint – you could let them use plastic gloves to avoid direct contact.

Discussion

What shape are the worms? Where do they live? Where do worms go? How do worms feel? How many worms have you got in your picture? Are there any long ones? Who eats worms? How long are most of the worms – use a ruler and some string to measure them.

Follow-up activities

✧ Put some cooked spaghetti into brown paint, then let the children feel it. Later, when it has dried, let the children put them 'underground' gluing them on brown paper.
✧ Use tubes and straws in the sand tray to make an environment of burrows, add Plasticine worms.
✧ Cover a climbing frame with blankets and simulate an environment that worms live in. Give the children torches for safety and allow them to explore in their 'wormery'.
✧ Make some wiggly worms using black or brown tights stuffed with paper, and display them on a large wall frieze.

LET'S TALK

Objective

English — To develop confidence in talking and to learn about conversation patterns.

Group size

Four to six children.

What you need

Simple puppets (made from two socks of different colours), scissors, buttons and felt scraps, needle and thread.

Preparation

Use the two socks as a basis to make simple puppets, sew the buttons onto the toe end of the sock to form the eyes, decorate with the scraps of felt to make a mouth.

I live below the ground

Hello, I'm Mr Worm

What to do

Start by modelling a question and answer conversation for the children.

Put one sock puppet onto your hand and introduce it as one of your worms, ask the children to give it a name. Let the children decide its character – is it a happy, sad, kind, bossy, angry or bad-tempered worm?

Set the scene for the activity by telling the children that one day the worm pops up from underground to take a look around. He hears crying; let the second 'worm' appear.

The first worm asks, 'Why are you so sad?' Use real events that have happened in your setting to promote discussion and give the children an opportunity to say what they think, removed from the actual situation.

As the children become competent develop more characters. Introduce them one by one and develop different personalities. Let the children use the puppets to interact and tell each other made-up stories.

Discussion

Use open-ended questions and allow the children to express their own ideas and feelings. How can you show the character of the puppet? Is it the face, clothes, voice or its actions? Why is the worm unhappy? Have you ever felt like that? What do you think the worm should do?

Follow-up activities

✧ Set up a role-play area of a 'Worms world'; replicate an underground environment using dark colours and confined spaces, make signs using worm-shaped letters.

✧ Let the children design and make their own worm puppets from socks and stick the features on. Use filled stockings and tights for extra long, flexible worms.

✧ Encourage the children to colour and cut out their own worm finger puppets using the photocopiable sheet on page 90.

WORMWATCH

Objective

Science – To construct a wormery so that children can observe and record scientific findings about worms.

Group size

Pairs, groups of four, individuals.

What you need

A jar / aquarium / container (with air holes), soil, leaves and vegetation, worms, black paper, sand, newspaper, dustpan and brush, plastic collecting container with lid, trowels, spades.

Preparation

Collect the resources together and ideally involve the children in the construction of the wormery. Go outside with the plastic containers, if possible after a rain shower. If that is not possible then bring out some spades and turn some earth over to find some worms. (Carefully lift up the worms and put them in the container. Put on the lid with air holes in.) Then make sure the children wash their hands.

What to do

Explain that the wormery is a place where the worms live, and that they have certain needs. Make layers of soil and sand in the large container for the wormery. Supervise the children whilst they pour in the materials, and shake each layer. Put the leaves and vegetation on the top layer.

Place the worms on the top layer and watch what they do. The children should observe how the worms burrow down into the soil until the last one goes underground.

Explain to the children that if you have earthworms in your garden you should have healthy plants, because the worms make the soil rich in oxygen and improve its moisture level.

Completely cover the container with black paper and place it on a table or suitable surface so it is at the children's height and they can observe it easily. They will be able to note slight changes in the following weeks.

Record the process of setting up the wormery through drawing and notes – make a note of the date. The layers will start to merge. Add vegetation regularly about every two days so that the worms can use it if they wish. Continue to observe the wormery until all the layers are mixed. Release the worms after the observation period (between two and three weeks) back into the environment.

Discussion

Where do you think worms live? (They live all over the world, but also in our gardens.) What do worms need? (They need a damp dark environment.) What do you think the worms do as they move up and down the layers? (They eat the soil and any bits not wanted pass through their bodies and they then make mounds or worm casts.) How does a worm move? (They move by stretching the front of their body and gripping to the soil with the hairs on their skin.) Are worms totally safe underground? (No, birds look for their casts and they pull them out of their burrows.)

Follow-up activities

✧ Put soil and sand in the sand try and use plastic or Plasticine worms, to create a small play environment.
✧ Make a concertina book with holes in each page and a ribbon worm that can be threaded through the book.
✧ Make a 2D picture of a wormery using a square of brown paper, Blu-Tack children's drawings of worms on it, and move them daily.

WIGGLY WORMS

• •

Objective

Mathematics – To compare lengths.

Group size

Six to eight children.

What you need

Cooked and dry spaghetti in different thicknesses. A large saucepan, cooker, trays, tongs, ribbon, string, elastic, a weak solution of washing-up liquid well diluted with water, a large hoop, an outside area of earth or grass.

Preparation

Cut the spaghetti into different lengths, divide into two piles and cook some of it. Put the raw pile onto one tray and heap the cold cooked spaghetti onto another one. Prepare the solution of washing-up liquid and put into a plastic bottle.

What to do

Take the children outside to observe the different sizes and shapes of worms (bearing in mind that worms usually only come out at night). Gently turn over a flower bed with a fork to find some worms. When you have successfully located some, observe together how they move. Afterwards, returning indoors make sure everyone washes their hands.

Use the different forms of spaghetti to represent the worms. Draw the children's attention to the different shapes and sizes. If some children do not like to touch the cold spaghetti then let them use the tongs.

Encourage the children to find the longest, the shortest, the thinnest or the fattest piece and let them sort it all according to size.

Finally let them sort the spaghetti worms according to their own criteria and ask the others to try to guess what it is.

Discussion

Worms move by contracting and stretching their muscular segments. They have fine bristles underneath the body that grip as they move along. Does the length of the worm always stay the same? Is it the same when it's curled up as when it's straightened out? How can you tell its length when it is curled up?

Follow-up activities

✧ Try to measure a piece of elastic; how long is it?
✧ Make paper worms and use string or ribbon to measure them exactly. Join the string to show the length of three worms, six worms or ten worms.
✧ Play 'Worm in the grass'. One child is the worm and lies on the ground pretending to be asleep. The other children creep up softly and gently touch the worm. When you clap your hands the worm wakes up and anyone who is touched by the worm has to lie down and also becomes a worm. Eventually everyone is 'tagged' and the ground is covered by wriggling worms.

SMALL WORLD

Objective

Geography – To plan and map an underground environment.

Group size

Pairs; small groups of six to eight children.

What you need

A large container such as a sand tray. Pieces of plumber's piping, paper, pencils and colouring pencils, adhesive, scissors, junk materials.

Preparation

The children should have had the opportunity of investigating and exploring where worms live or observing them in a wormery.

What to do

Explain to the children that they are going to make a pretend place where worms would like to live, work and play. They will need to think about the features to put in and what the worms need. Let the children design the play area on paper, mapping out and labelling the areas. Talk about their design ideas clarifying how things work and where things are placed.

When they are satisfied with their plans let them use the sand tray to make their worm environment, using the pipes and junk materials.

Discussion

Use the children's knowledge of worms to focus on what they will need. Ask, how are worms different to humans, how do they move? (Tunnel, slither, slide, stretch and curl.) What do they think the worms need to do? (Tunnel and move soil about, eat the dead plant material in the soil, find moisture.) Do they like the light or the dark? (Dark.) Damp or dry? (Damp.) What sort of textures do you think they would like – rough, smooth, knobbly, shiny? (The bristles underneath their bodies help them to grip as they move along.) Do you think they can swim – will they need a pool? (Some worms live in the water, but they are still usually anchored in burrows on the bottom.) Do they live alone or in groups? (They live in groups, in underground tunnels.)

Follow-up activities

✧ Make an obstacle course with the PE apparatus. Cover some with drapes or blankets to create dark spaces and let the children worm their way around; use the words up, over, under and along the ground as they wiggle.
✧ Experiment to see if worms like wet or dry conditions. Prepare different surfaces, dry, damp and wet; observe which the worms prefer.
✧ Find out if worms prefer light or dark places.

GARDENER'S FRIEND

Objective

RE – To understand that all living things have a purpose.

Group size

Four to six children.

What you need

Access to a patch of earth, grass or rough ground. Soil, sand, trowels, forks, small buckets for each pair of children, a large transparent container, rope and poles or a large PE hoop, black paper, a 3D viewer and hand lens.

Preparation

Mark off a section of the earth with the hoop/rope about one metre square. Have one section for each pair of children. Fill the large container with alternate layers of soil and damp sand.

What to do

Explain to the children that all living things have a role on earth and you are going outside to investigate how worms are useful and how they help us.

Tell the children that they burrow in the soil, mixing it and aerating it. They eat their way through the soil, pulling dead leaves into it. They are food for birds and other creatures. A football pitch could have two million worms tunnelling away keeping the soil fresh!

Let children work in pairs to dig in their section of soil. Encourage them to look for worms. Bear in mind that some children may feel timid about handling worms and they shouldn't be forced to if they are reluctant. When you have collected some worms put them in the prepared container and cover with grass and dead leaves. Take them indoors, cover the container with black paper and leave for a few days. Remove the paper and see how the worms have mixed up the sand and soil. Worms will come to the surface for food but they don't like bright light. Return the worms where you found them and make sure the children all wash their hands.

Discussion

Some children may not like worms, yet will still understand that they are good for the soil and help plants grow. Do you like worms? What do you think worms like to eat and drink? What do you think the worms do in the soil? How does it help the gardener or the farmer to have worms in the soil? (It breaks up the soil and helps plants to grow.) What does the soil feel like – is it wet, damp, dry, thick, sticky, soft, fine? What would the earth be like if the worms didn't break up the soil? Why wouldn't plants grow so easily?

Follow-up activities

✧ Link with other activities on helping each other.
✧ Make books with lift-up flaps – what's under here?
✧ Try different materials in the sand tray and see which is easiest for tunnelling.
✧ Make a close observation of a worm and paint a picture of it, matching the marking and colouring.

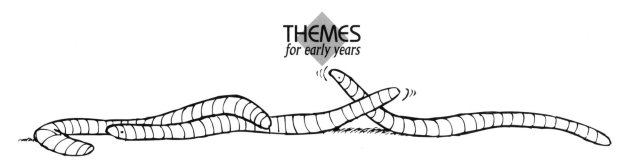

THE TALE OF THE WORM

Objective

English – To develop sentence writing skills.

Group size

Six children.

What you need

Paper, pencils, scissors, pieces of card in green or brown, felt-tipped pen.

Preparation

Ensure that the children have had the opportunity to observe real worms. Cut out a worm-shaped piece of paper for each child, these can be different shapes and sizes, wiggly, straight, fat or thin. Prepare six sets of word cards with the following words: A, a, worm, worms, can, has, have.

What to do

Explain to the group that they are each going to write a sentence about a worm on the worm-shaped paper. Make sure they understand where the beginning and the end of the sentence will be.

Brainstorm what the children know about worms. Ask them to give you any words they can think of and write them all down. Look for descriptive words and write these

key words on pieces of card. Show and say the words in the prepared word sets to the children as well.

Let the children shuffle the word cards around to make a sentence. Supply any other words they may need on pieces of card. Once they are happy with their sentence they can write it onto the paper worm. Point out that each sentence starts with a capital letter and finishes with a full stop. Show the children where these will be.

The children in your group may be at quite different stages of writing ability. Observe what each child can write unaided and celebrate their achievements. Their free, independent writing and drawing attempts will provide valuable information about their understanding and skills of writing. This information can be used to develop and extend their language learning.

When the children have finished, display the six different sentences on a background of paper grass or earth-coloured paper.

Discussion

Ask, at which end of the paper worm will your sentence start? What have you found out about worms? What can your eyes tell you about a worm?

Follow-up activities

✧ Encourage the children to cut out their own worm shapes and write more sentences.

✧ Use the word cards to make a group poem about worms.

✧ Make up a story about a little lonely worm who keeps getting lost. Make a long concertina book showing his journey and his adventures.

✧ Use a bunch of knotted string as a maze. Can you sort it out?

SLITHER AND SLIDE

Objective

PE — To explore the movement of their own bodies in space.

Group size

Eight to ten children.

What you need

A large area where the children can be free to move. Four or five tables, dark coloured drapes or blankets. The finger poem 'A tiny, tiny worm' from page 74.

Preparation

The children should be comfortably dressed or changed into loose clothing so that they can move freely, they should wear plimsolls or have bare feet. Space the tables around the room and spread the drapes over them to make dark spaces.

What to do

Gather the children around you and set the atmosphere. If possible, darken the room. Say the finger poem 'A tiny, tiny worm'.

Tell the children they have become worms and have entered an underground world. Let each child find a dark place under a table. Make sure the children are spaced out well, two to a table. Ask them to close their eyes and move slowly around the floor. Remind them they are worms and they should try to move without using their hands or arms. This will give exercise to their large trunk muscles. Bring variety into their movements by asking the children to move slowly, quickly, lightly or quietly.

End the session by asking them to be very still and not to move a muscle. Then tell them to open their eyes. In this activity the children will experience moving their bodies in relation to the space available. Some children may not feel comfortable in a small dark space so let them choose an open space in which to move around.

Discussion

Ask them to tell you what it felt like to be in the dark space. How easy is it to move without arms and legs? Let them describe the different sort of movements they made — wriggle, squirm, slither and slide. How did they keep from bumping into each other?

Follow-up activities

✧ Make a 'worm obstacle course' with PE apparatus concentrating on wriggling — use concertina tunnels and hoops and other circular items that link to 'tunnels'.
✧ Make a wormery world using large play equipment of tunnels and tubes.
✧ Make pathways, trails, routes with small apparatus and ropes for the children to follow.
✧ Give each child a copy of the photocopiable sheet 'Wormery maze', page 91 to develop fine motor control.

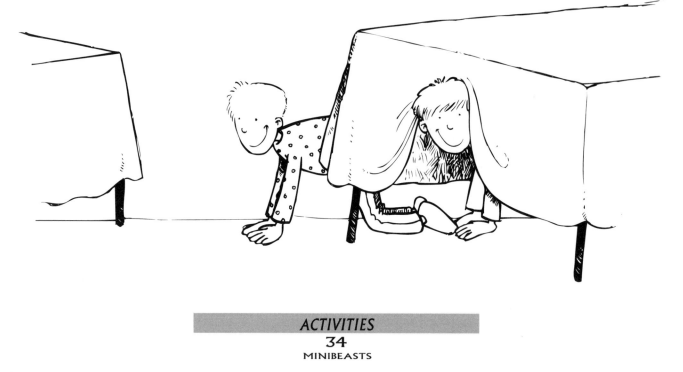

CHAPTER 4
SPIDERS

Weave a web with craft materials and with skipping ropes and bodies in a PE activity! Write some spider poems and play the spider board game to complete the topic.

SPIDER GAME

Objective

Mathematics — To match and compare using mathematical skills such as counting and size comparisons.

Group size

Two to four children.

What you need

Spider templates of varying size, (or use plastic spiders), card, scissors, a large piece of white cardboard, felt-tipped pens, pencils, a dice.

Preparation

Use the large piece of white cardboard as a baseboard, draw a large cobweb in the centre of the card and smaller ones around the edge. Draw a pathway from each of the small cobwebs to the centre cobweb. Divide the pathways and mark segments with numbers one to ten. Collect the plastic spider counters or make spider counters using templates.

What to do

Explain to the children how to play the game: they start by each putting their spiders in one of the small webs. To play they take turns to throw the dice and move their spiders the number of places shown on the dice towards the centre. The aim is to take their spiders 'home' to the larger web. At the end of the game they need to throw the exact number to finish on the large web. Play the game until all the spiders get back into the web.

Explain to the children that they must count the numbers on the dice carefully and then at the end of the game they need to get the correct number to finish.

Discussion

Which spider is the biggest? Can you count the number line to the centre? Which spider will get there first? Do all spiders live in webs? Which spider spun the central web?

Follow-up activities

✧ Use a dice which has weather symbols on: a sun, rain, a cloud, snow. Ask the children to sing 'Incy Wincy Spider' and move the counters up if the weather is good, if it is bad move down one square.

✧ Photocopy the card / plastic spiders several times. Make a number line with the spiders, writing the numbers one to five and under each number placing the correct amount of spiders.

✧ Mix large and small spider shapes and ask the children to sort and count.

✧ Using the fact that a spider has eight legs make number bonds to add up to eight: $1 + 7$, $6 + 2$, $5 + 3$ and $4 + 4$.

POETRY WEB

Objective

English — To use the theme of spiders as a stimulus for poetry, using real or imaginative experiences, feelings and fears about spiders.

Group size

Small groups, pairs and individuals.

What you need

Some real spiders to look at, pictures of spiders, books, poems and rhymes about spiders, A4 paper, pencils or pens, a large sheet of paper on which to record initial thoughts.

Preparation

Display all the stimulus material. Try to provide a quiet working area for the children to focus and concentrate on their poems.

What to do

Explain that just by looking at a spider you can see and perhaps feel lots of different things. In turns ask the children to tell you what they see or feel and record their thoughts on a large piece of paper. Point out the difference between an observation and a feeling. If the children run out of ideas of their own read some poems to them such as 'I heard a spider sobbing' or 'Spider in the bath' taken from *Big Billy* by Peter Dixon (Peter Dixon Books), or see pages 67, 70 and 73.

Let the children work in small groups, in pairs or individually using the collected ideas. The poetry could be written on plain paper or if the children want to present their ideas in different ways provide some 'spider shaped' paper. If the

children find the writing process difficult, then an adult can scribe it, so that their imaginative ideas are captured.

When all the poems are complete display them on a large 'poetry web'.

Discussion

What do you think/feel about spiders? What words could you use to describe them? How do they move? Their webs are very carefully constructed, where would you find them? Are spiders frightened of any other minibeasts?

Follow-up activities

✧ Make a group spider poetry collection in a zigzag book.
✧ Photocopy some plastic spiders, make a border on sheets of paper for the children to use to write some further poetry.
✧ Make/buy some spider puppets and use speech bubbles, ask the children what the spiders would say or feel.

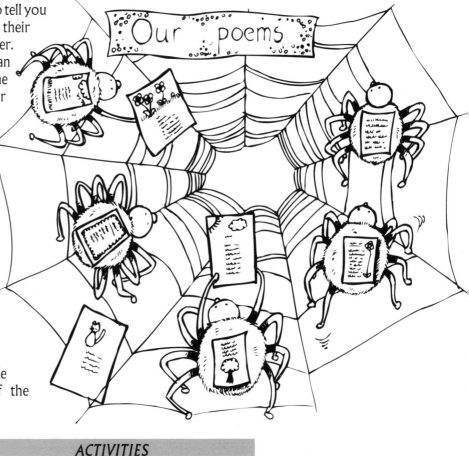

WEAVE A WEB

Objective

Design and Technology – To design and construct a spider's web, using weaving and lacing skills.

Group size

Four to six children.

What you need

A collection of string, threads, wools, short garden canes or plant support sticks (eight per child), scissors, pictures or photographs showing spiders' webs.

Preparation

Lay out the range of threads, wools and so on so that the children can see, feel and touch the variety of items.

What to do

Explain to the children how carefully a spider weaves a web, that it takes time and it is carefully designed. Look at some pictures or photos of spiders' webs.

Tie or lace the eight canes or sticks like a star shape by securing the centre with strong string. You may find it easier to work on four sticks and then add others when this is secure. Once the base of the web is ready then begin by tying a piece of thread and then twisting and wrapping the thread around the sticks in a circular manner. Begin in the centre of the sticks and work outwards.

As the children get further out then try and tie on the cane higher up and let the thread lay loosely so that the shape of a web is imitated.

The web can be made in one colour or as a colourful mixture. Using different threads will give the children an opportunity to explore the different qualities of the threads and strings in terms of thickness, strengths and flexibility.

Discussion

Which way does a spider spin its web? (The web consists of a 'sheet' of threads and sinks in the centre, rather like a hammock. Careful investigation will show that in one corner the web is formed like a funnel.) Do spiders eat every day like us? (No, they do not need to feed regularly. They can go without food for a long time.) Which thread/wool is the most like a spider's web and why? How do you move the web as you work? Which is the hardest part to do and why? Does a spider ever make a mistake?

Follow-up activities

✧ Make a 'dream catcher', weaving using a circle instead of a star shape.
✧ Use old rust-free wheels with spokes to weave threads and rags in and out of.
✧ Make a web pattern on paper using a glue stick and sprinkle glitter on top, or use glitter pens.
✧ Make webs using black wool glued onto paper, then photocopy these and look at each child's attempt. How many are different, how many are the same?

SPIDER SEQUENCE

Objective

PE/Drama – To move like spiders making webs.

Group size

Eight children.

What you need

Skipping ropes (at least one per child), adequate and suitable space, cassette recorder, taped music such as the *Superman* theme.

Preparation

The children should be comfortably dressed or change into loose clothing so that they can move freely, wear plimsolls or have bare feet. Tell the children it is important to warm up before exercising and begin by asking the children to run gently on the spot and then in and out of the spaces in the designated area. Using the skipping ropes, lay a rope on the ground and jump to either side to warm up.

What to do

Tell the children that they are going to make giant spider webs using skipping ropes. Ask six of the children to get into pairs to tie their skipping ropes together to make a star shape. The other two children should take different positions, one in the middle of the star and the other on the outside.

Explain to the two children that they need to move under and over the ropes, pretending to be busy spiders weaving a

web. Ask the six rope holders to kneel or bend down to make this easier. Try this without the music first and let the children have plenty of practice.

Make regular changes so that the rope holders have a turn at weaving.

To finish, let the spiders (the moving children) dance around the room and when the music stops they have to go to the middddle of the web.

Discussion

How do spiders move? Do they twist and turn or just go up and down? (Spiders make webs that consist of sheets of thread and sinks in the centre, rather like a hammock. Point out to the children that although spiders webs are strong enough to catch a fly they can easily be destoyed by a finger.) Can they move fast or slow? If you move quickly what must you remember? What would happen if I was a fly and I came into the web? (If a fly is caught in the web then the spider will come out and eat its prey.)

Follow-up activities

✧ Make up a spider dance linked with weather using the rhyme 'Incy Wincy Spider' as a stimulus.
✧ Act out the roles of a spider and a fly!
✧ Make spider masks using gold or silver thread; make a large scale web using hammer, nails and a large piece of chipboard.
✧ Use tent pegs and ropes outside on grass to make a giant web.

SPIDER STORIES

• •

Objective

RE – To learn stories from other cultures.

Group size

Up to eight children.

What you need

A story book containing one of the Anansi tales (see Recommended Materials on page 96), which come from the West African and Caribbean tradition. They tell tales of a crafty trickster, a man who is able to change into a spider (Anansi is a West African word for spider). Card, paper, felt-tipped pens or crayons, Blu-Tack.

Preparation

Prepare a comfortable area where the children are able to listen to the story. Cut the card into labels large enough to write on.

What to do

Read the chosen story of Anansi to the children and discuss the sort of person he is in the story. Many of the stories show him to be a clever trickster who gets what he wants at the expense of others (*Anansi and the tiger stories*). Sometimes he comes off badly because he is too greedy (*Anansi and the yams*).

Think of words to describe Anansi's personal qualities and how the

other animals perceive him (often they expect him to do bad things).

Discuss with the children the qualities they personally would like to have. Try to encourage positive contributions such as: gentle, funny, good, happy, kind. Write these words on the labels. Find as many words as possible.

Next let the children each make a portrait of themselves (using paints or crayons) and ask the other children to choose one of the cards to describe their friend and attach it to the portrait with Blu-Tack.

Emphasise that we are all different and unique. Be sensitive to individual children in your group and be aware of any special problem areas or subjects. Emphasise that a very special quality is to be sensitive to other people's feelings.

Discussion

Ask the children to think about the story and decide what sort of person Anansi is. What do other characters in the story say about him? What sort of qualities do we look for in people? What do you do when someone has been nasty, unkind, mean to you? How does it make us feel when someone is kind to us?

Follow-up activities

✧ Construct Anansi spider figures from recycled or modelling materials.
✧ Encourage a sense of identity by illustrating the children's portraits with pictures showing their particular interests and skills.
✧ Introduce self-esteem work and circle time to the group.

LONG AGO LEGENDS

. . . .

Objective

History – To learn about the past through stories.

Group size

Eight to ten children.

What you need

The story of Robert Bruce (a brief outline is found on page 81), pictures of winter/summer in the Scottish Highlands, shoebox, adhesive, scissors, card, recycled materials for model making.

Preparation

Mount the pictures onto thin card. Prepare for the modelling activity.

What to do

Read the children the story and show pictures of the Highlands. Talk about the sort of place where Robert Bruce had to stay and hide out during the winter. Contrast with holidays or visits the children have made away from home.

Ask the children to use the recycled modelling materials to make a hut and some of the things Robert Bruce would have used for fishing and hunting such as dishes for food, pots to carry water, covers and blankets.

Discussion

Have any of the children been to the Highlands. What was it like? How was it different long ago? How did Robert and his men get there. (Walked and rode horses.) What is a hut? How different is it to a house? What did they sleep on? (Animal skins, straw mattresses.) Where did they get food? (Gathering berries, hunting and fishing.) Why did Robert Bruce have to stay in the hut? (He was hoping the English king wouldn't find him there.) Why did he wait until spring? Contrast the story with life today where we have different kinds of transport, hotels, supermarkets, telephones and TV to tell us the news.

Follow-up activities

✧ Read other stories that use spiders in a positive way, such as *Charlotte's Web* by E. B. White (Penguin), and on video.
✧ Look at different kinds of shelters we use today and look for ways to keep warm in cold weather.
✧ Use the pictures of the Scottish Highlands as a stimulus for a painting activity. Compare the pictures to the area in which the children live.

SPIDER SPY

Objective

Science — To know that living things can be grouped according to observable similarities and differences.

Group size

Four to six children.

What you need

A spider, a transparent collecting jar (there are specially made spider catchers but you can simply cover the spider with a container and then slide under a lid, muslin or gauze), hand lens, paper, colouring pencils.

Preparation

First gently catch your spider and keep it in a transparent container covering the top with a piece of muslin or gauze.

What to do

Encourage the children to watch the spider in the container, or alternatively you could observe spiders outside on bushes and grass, or search for them in doorways, gardens, sheds and corners. On autumn mornings point out dew-covered webs to the children.

Use a hand lens to closely observe the spider, watching how it moves. Encourage the children to describe the shape of the body and where the legs are positioned. Let the children close their eyes and try to remember the shape of the spider, then look again.

Talk about the food chain and how different animals rely on eating other animals in order to survive. Explain that garden spiders are coloured to blend in with their surroundings because birds look for them to eat. Some spiders can eat frogs and birds but the ones which we see usually eat small insects which they catch by trapping them in their webs. Explain that the house spider doesn't use a web to catch its prey, it just pounces!

Ask the children to finish by drawing a spider a place in which it likes to live.

Discussion

Ask the children how they know it is a spider in the container. (A spider is not an insect. It has eight legs and doesn't have wings.) Do spiders all look the same? (There are thousands of spiders in the world. They are in many different colours and sizes.) Talk about where you found your spider. Where do spiders live and what do they use the webs for? (Most spiders spin webs to catch their prey.) How do the webs catch the insects? (The webs have a sticky covering. Once the insect is trapped in the web the spider feels the vibration on the thread and comes to get the insect.) Is a spider useful? (Yes it eats many of the insects which would eat crops.) Can it harm you? (Although spiders have a poison in their fangs only a few could actually harm a human. Most of these do not live in the UK.)

Follow-up activities

✧ Find out which other creatures have eight legs.
✧ Read the pop-up book by Jan Pienkowski, *Fancy that* (Orchard Books).
✧ Visit a zoo and look at exotic spiders.

THERE'S A SPIDER!

Objective

RE – To explore different feelings and to consider other people's feelings.

Group size

Small group of four to six children.

What you need

The song 'Spiders' (page 87), coloured felt-tipped pens, a small paper plate for each child, a mirror.

Preparation

Practise the song together.

What to do

Talk about the way the spider is presented in the words of the song and how sometimes spiders are shown as menacing and frightening. Discuss the things the spider can do such as spin a delicate web and walk on the ceiling. Mention to the children how useful a spider is to the environment by eating flies which breed disease.

Talk about the different words that can be used to describe feelings such as frightened, scared, happy, glad, angry or jealous. Let the children take it in turns to look in the mirror and explore different facial expressions, what happens to their faces when they smile, frown, look sad or laugh?

Ask the children to remember something that happened to them that made them happy. Now let them make pictures of their happy face on their paper plates.

End the session by playing 'catch a smile'. Sit in a circle, one child looks at another, makes eye contact and smiles. That child 'takes' the smile, looks at someone else and passes it on! Continue around the group until everyone is smiling.

Discussion

Ask the children why people are frightened of spiders. Do you think spiders will hurt us? (Explain that very few spiders can harm humans, most of these live in hot countries.) What makes you feel afraid? How do you feel when you are afraid, what

do you do? Do you want to run and play, sit still and be quiet or hide? What do you do when you see someone is sad or upset? How can you make someone else feel better or happy? Discuss the good things that have happened, things which make the children feel happy. Some children may wish to confide in you and disclose unpleasant things that have happened to them. *Do* be accessible and receptive, listen carefully and take them seriously. Reassure the child and if necessary get further help and advice and make a careful record of what was said.

Follow-up activities

✧ Sing the song 'If you're happy and you know it'.
✧ Read *It's too frightening for me* by Shirley Hughes (Young Puffin Books).
✧ Play 'Spiders and Sparrows' by marking out two lines, three metres apart. The children stand on line A, bend down and put their hands on the ground with their backs to line B. On a signal they quickly move backwards to reach line B, once they cross that line they hop forwards to line A.
✧ Say the rhyme 'Little Miss Muffet'. Ask the children how the spider felt when she ran away.

CHAPTER 5
BUTTERFLIES

Observe the change from caterpillar to butterfly with ideas in this chapter including making clay butterflies, symmetrical butterfly prints and trying out the caterpillar crawl!

CATERPILLAR CHANGES

Objective

Science – To learn how living things grow and change.

Group size

Six to eight children.

What you need

Paper, colouring pens, scissors, children's information books such as *The Caterpillar Story* (Evans), a transparent container such as a sweet jar with a lid (punch out air holes in the lid), some fresh leaves, photocopiable page 92 one per child.

Preparation

The change from caterpillar to butterfly may take up to a month, so plan to introduce it when you and the children have had time to observe the changes. April or May should be a good time to find some eggs or caterpillars. Look on nettles, grasses, bushes and oak trees for caterpillars (or their eggs) and collect them together with a good supply of green leaves (collected) from where the caterpillar was feeding (if you don't provide the right kind of leaf the caterpillar may die). Place in the container. Prepare a paper circle for each child and divide each one into four sections.

What to do

Explain to the children as simply as possible the change of a caterpillar to a butterfly. Use children's information books such as *The Caterpillar Story* to support what you are explaining.

Watch the caterpillars feed and grow. Talk about the changes as they occur and let the children draw each stage in the quarters of their paper circle.

Eventually the skin will split (this can happen four times), and after three or four months the caterpillar is ready to turn into a chrysalis. Watch the chrysalis develop; this is a safe case where the pupa changes and develops. Wait and watch for the emerging butterfly. Encourage the children to use the correct vocabulary – pupa, cocoon, chrysalis. Explain that metamorphosis means to change shape. Set the butterfly free as soon as possible.

Finish by using photocopiable page 92 with the children. Let them work alone or with a partner to sequence the pictures correctly.

Discussion

How is the pupa different to the caterpillars? What does it feel like? Why does the caterpillar shed its skin? Do other insects go through this change? (Bees, ants, beetles.) What do you think is happening inside the chrysalis? Why do you think they make this change? The caterpillar crawls but once it's a butterfly it can fly. If you could change what would you like to be?

Follow-up activities

✧ Compare the human life cycle with the butterfly. How do we change? What can you do now that you couldn't when you were a baby? What happens to us as we get older?
✧ Look at how animations are made; mark a piece of paper into twelve numbered sections and draw the caterpillar changing shape to become a butterfly. In section one draw the caterpillar and in section twelve the butterfly. Fill in the other sections to show the changes.
✧ Attract butterflies by planting buddleia, lilac and sweet-william plants.

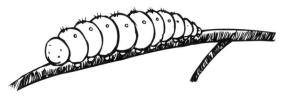

FIND THE BUTTERFLY!

Objective

Mathematics – To match and correspond shapes and silhouettes and develop spatial awareness.

Group size

Four to six children.

What you need

A large piece of card (at least 60cm × 60cm), a collection of pictures of butterflies (from wrapping paper or colouring books), adhesive, scissors, black paper, paints or felt-tipped pens.

Preparation

Cut out the butterfly shapes accurately. Carefully trace the picture outlines onto the black paper and cut these out to produce a silhouette for each butterfly. Split the originals and the silhouettes into two piles. On the large piece of card either paint or draw with felt-tipped pens some large garden flowers and glue on the butterfly pictures to form a baseboard.

What to do

Tell the children to look very carefully at the baseboard pictures. Take the pile of black paper cut-outs and lay it down near the baseboard. Ask the children to look carefully at the shapes and sizes of the butterflies. Ask them to decide which silhouette matches each butterfly and to lay it on top of the relevant picture. If they get it wrong let the next child in the group have a try.

Try at the design stage to get several butterfly pictures that are similar, in order to challenge the children. If the game is too easy you can always add some more butterflies overnight and see if the children notice! Once all the butterflies have been matched, extend the activity by asking the children to put them in order of largest to smallest. Note how similar the shape of the butterfly is whatever the size and let the children fold the silhouettes in half to see the symmetry.

Discussion

What do you look at when you have to match? How can you check you have matched correctly? A butterfly has a special shape, what is special about it? (It is symmetrical.) What other things are symmetrical? Do butterflies fly at night? (No, but moths do.)

Follow-up activities

✧ Let the children make their own matching butterfly board.
✧ Hand out photocopiable page 93 and ask the children to look hard to find all the butterflies and caterpillars hidden on the page. Let them colour the shapes in and then count up how many of each they can find.
✧ Photocopy pieces of jigsaws and ask the children to sort and find the correct pieces that match.

A DAY IN THE LIFE

Objective

History – To put events into a simple time sequence and to develop 'time' vocabulary.

Group size

Four to six children.

What you need

Lengths of card to fold into a zigzag of at least four or six pages, large sheet of paper, felt-tipped pens (or wrapping paper with some colourful butterflies), scissors, pencils, adhesive, A4 paper, a collection of commercial zigzag books, *The Very Hungry Caterpillar* by Eric Carle (Hamish Hamilton).

Preparation

Collect some zigzag books to show/use as a template. Allow plenty of horizontal space for working on. Read a suitable story such as *The Very Hungry Caterpillar* by Eric Carle. The purpose of this activity is not to copy the story, but to help the children to sequence a set of events and to use appropriate 'time' vocabulary.

What to do

Explain that the children are each going to think carefully about making a special book about butterflies, it could be a story book and/or information book. They can 'illustrate' the book or use cut out pictures, emphasise that the choice is theirs because they are the authors of the books.

Look at how zigzag books are designed. Invite the children to construct their books themselves. Lay a published book flat to use as a template and fold it in the correct places.

Once the zigzag base is constructed, talk about the beginning, the middle and the end of the story. On a large sheet of paper, draw out the story of a butterfly in sequence: the first page will be a butterfly laying an egg on a leaf; then the eggs hatching into a caterpillar; then the caterpillar changing into a chrysalis and finally the chrysalis changing into a butterfly. Explain how the cycle begins again. Ask the children to draw this sequence out in their books. Use the opportunity to develop the children's understanding of the passage of time, drawing parallels to the changes in their lives.

Once the picture designs are organised, then the words need to be written. This may be done in a variety of ways, depending on the ability of the child. The child may be confident to try unaided, asking for help with difficult spellings or may need an adult to scribe or copy from.

Once the books are complete make sure the children make a title and write their name on it like real authors.

Discussion

What happens first in the sequence? How does it end? What pictures do you need? How do you know where to start or finish? Is the book an information book or a story book? Who is the author of the book?

Follow-up activities

✧ Make a small zigzag book to fit in your pocket.
✧ Play some card sequencing games.
✧ Use a well-known story to act out; but change one part of it.

BUTTERFLY GARDEN

Objective

RE – To understand that living things need care and attention.

Group size

Four to six children.

What you need

An area of garden or a collection of plant pots, plants that encourage butterflies (such as buddleia, french marigolds and alyssum), a watering can, a butterfly reference book, trowels, spades, paper and pencil, a camera (optional).

Preparation

If possible visit a garden centre together to look at and purchase the plants. Identify the area where the plants are to be planted, check that the conditions are suitable.

What to do

Carefully look at the plants and read the information about the needs of plants and where to site them. Let the children see that the plants need to be held gently. Dig the site with the children, talking about the minibeasts you may come across. Explain how it is important to care for all living things.

Plant and water the butterfly garden. Observe the plants and try to identify all the butterflies that visit the plants. Photograph or draw the butterflies and keep a diary of the sightings.

Draw up a timetable for the children to water the plants, check them, weed the area of ground/pot. Measuring the growth of the plants will also indicate that the plants are settled.

Discussion

What do the plants need? (Light, heat and food.) What happens to butterflies in autumn if they do not hibernate? (They die, but they leave eggs behind.) What colour are the plants that butterflies are attracted to? (Bright colours such as pink, lilac and yellow.)

Follow-up activities

✧ Use a reference book and make a list of butterflies actually seen on the plants.
✧ Look out for caterpillars at the appropriate time of year.
✧ Keep a diary of how the butterfly garden was set up; invite parents to donate butterfly plants.
✧ Take photographs of butterflies to display with any of the children's work.

BUTTERFLY DOUBLE

Objective

Art – To explore symmetry, colour and patterns.

Group size

Small group size, four to six children.

What you need

Paint, scissors, collage materials (cloth, textured material), adhesive, string, pictures of butterflies, A4 paper, ruler.

Preparation

Invite the children to look at the pictures of the butterflies, then cover half the picture up with a book so that they focus on one side of the butterfly only. Arrange the materials so that the children can select what they may need.

What to do

Fold the pictures of the butterflies in half and discuss how the butterflies are symmetrical. Point out that this is something that you will be able to show at the end of the activity.

Give each child a sheet of A4 paper, fold it in half and select one half to work on. Show the children how to draw the outline of half of the butterfly and then how to glue and stick on string over the outline; leave it to dry. Use pieces of textured material or cloth, cutting out the pattern and colours required and fill in the details using these collage materials.

Next add a coat of fairly thick paint over the whole surface of the half butterfly, fold the paper over on top of it and press down firmly on the collaged side. Show the children that the print that occurs on the other half is a reflection of the decorated butterfly.

When the butterflies are dry, use a ruler to draw a dotted line vertically to indicate the line of symmetry. Display the completed butterflies flying on your walls.

Discussion

What kinds of patterns can you see? What colours are on the butterfly? Are the patterns the same each side of the butterfly? If the print does not come out what should you do? Butterflies sometimes have names that tell us what they look like such as cabbage white or red admiral. What could you call your butterfly?

Follow-on activities

✧ Display pictures of other symmetrical items.
✧ Print with other objects – which of these could be symmetrical?
✧ Make felt butterflies by folding felt over, cutting out the butterfly shape, then gluing on sequins, pieces of net and other materials. Make both sides identical.
✧ Make a matching game: choose some symmetrical objects but only draw half of the picture. Use a mirror placed vertically or horizontally to get the whole picture.

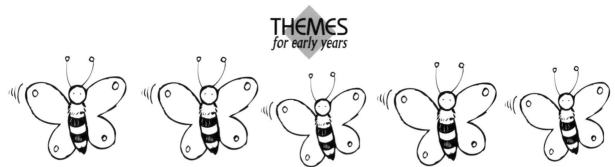

BEAUTIFUL BUTTERFLY

Objective

Design and Technology — To explore shape and form based on observation.

Group size

Four children.

What you need

Clay for each child: red earthenware clay is inexpensive, or use buff clay if you want to paint the masks later (do not mix red and buff together), roller, modelling tools (lolly sticks, spatulas, spoons, forks), plastic bags, small bowl of water and a sponge, a yoghurt pot and thin paintbrush, plenty of newspaper, hessian base cloths or boards to work on to prevent the clay from sticking, aprons, string, PVA adhesive/ varnish.

Preparation

Protect the working area with plenty of newspaper as clay work can become messy. Prepare by cutting the clay in advance, slice a portion of clay for each child, put it in a plastic bag and secure it tightly. Prepare a workstation for each child with a baseboard or mat to work on, roller, tools and a lump of clay. Children need to keep their hands moist, not wet, whilst working with clay; provide a damp sponge for them to press their hands on. Children should have had the opportunity of observing butterflies.

What to do

Explain to the children they are going to make a butterfly head using clay. Observe butterflies or pictures of them and talk about the shape and the position of the large compound eyes and the antennae, which are very sensitive and used to feel, smell and taste things. Point out the proboscis, this is the long curling tube that is used to suck up their food (nectar).

If the children have not used clay before let them experiment with it first. Can they pull it, stretch it, squeeze it? Let them roll and flatten it then show them how to roll it out like a pancake about 1cm thick. Make sure they keep it in one piece. When they have a good sized piece, cut and trim the shape of a butterfly's face and cut out holes for the eyes. Next take a smaller piece of clay and roll out a long thin piece to form the feelers and proboscis. Attach them to the pancake shape by making clay glue (a mixture of clay and water) to smear onto both surfaces. Curl up the end of the proboscis. Using one of the tools make small holes either side of the face to make fixing holes so that when the clay is dry a string can be threaded through. The children may like to decorate the faces by making marks and incising patterns in the clay. Build up a wedge of newspapers to form a mound and gently pass the clay over it. This will hold the clay whilst it is drying, to form a 3D shape.

The clay will take about a week to dry out fully, it can then be coated with PVA adhesive or varnish.

Discussion

Did you enjoy working with the clay? How was it different to other modelling material such as Plasticine or play dough? How was it the same?

Follow-up activities

✧ Use the clay butterfly face as a mould. Cover it first with protective film and then paste on five or six layers of glue-soaked paper. Once dry remove from the mould and decorate.
✧ Explore other materials such as Mod Roc (a commercially produced plaster bandage) or try winding fabric dipped in adhesive around a wire frame.

THE UGLY BUG BALL

Objective

Music – To respond to music and use imagination.

Group size

Six to eight children.

What you need

A recording of the song 'The ugly bug ball', recorded by Michael Feinstein (on *Pure imagination* from Elektra), cassette recorder, paper and pencils, an overhead projector, OHP pens, transparent acetate, a blank wall or large sheet as a projection screen.

Preparation

Have the music ready to play. Prepare the screen by pinning the sheet to the wall.

What to do

Sit the children down comfortably and listen to the music together. Switch off and ask the children to 'listen' to it again inside their heads; can they remember any parts? Now listen to it again.

As the children listen to the music, give them the OHP pens and the transparent sheets and let them use the pens to draw pictures of the ugly bugs which they can imagine from the music. Switch on the OHP and project the pictures onto the wall or the screen to tell the story of the ugly bug ball. Let the children practise moving the focus and the distance of the OHP to create the illusion of movement on the screen.

Plan out a storyboard to show the sequence of the images to accompany the music. Ask the children to identify which image will come first, then next, then which one will finish the song.

Discussion

Can the children identify which passages of the music have a regular rhythm. Is the music fast or slow? Are the notes high or low? Can the children recognise the structure of the song, the beginning, middle and end? Are any passages repeated? Is there a chorus? How many pictures will be needed for the length of the song? How quickly or how slowly will they be changed?

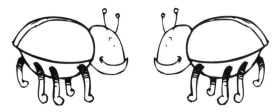

Follow-up activities

✧ Explore ways of making sounds using everyday objects: plucking, hitting, shaking.
✧ Use simple percussion instruments (or home-made ones) to make sounds to represent the butterfly flitting from flower to flower or emerging from a cocoon, caterpillars munching on leaves or moving along a branch.
✧ Project the OHP images onto the children's bodies (dressed in white) as they dance.

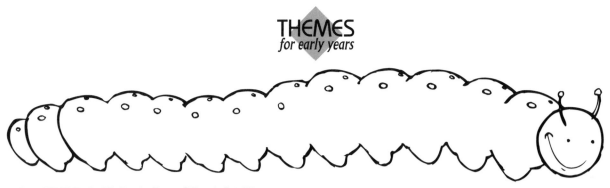

CATERPILLAR CRAWL

Objective

PE – To explore different ways of travelling.

Group size

Whole group/class.

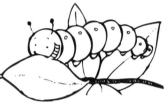

What you need

The song 'Caterpillar munch' (see page 83), ideally on tape so that the children can move to the music, a large free space, some simple percussion instruments (some to make a high sound, some a low sound), floor mats.

Preparation

The children should be comfortably dressed or change into loose clothing so that they can move freely, wear plimsolls or have bare feet. Place the floor mats around the room leaving space to move in between. The children should have had the opportunity to observe the movements of butterflies and caterpillars. Explain that the mats are leaves in a garden.

What to do

Learn the song together and let the children explore moving in different ways following the words in the song; munching here, munching there, spinning and then flying like the butterfly all around the garden.

Now, begin by asking the children to walk all around the room, tell them that you are going to make either a high sound or a low sound and to be ready to listen. Tell the children when they hear the high sound they must reach high above their heads and float their arms down again to their sides and gently dance around between the mats then come to rest on a 'leaf' mat, very still.

On the low note they should lie face down on a mat and move like a caterpillar, pulling their bodies forward with their hands. Finally raise the trunk to a kneeling position and bring the hands slowly up the whole body past the chest and ears and extend above the head ready to be a butterfly again. Look out for:

butterflies – lightness of movement and good use of the space with faster movements – a good starting position, hands above the head and a good finishing position, being still on the mat.

caterpillars – stretching and curling on the mat, slower, controlled movements. Use your voice to control the s-t-r-e-t-c-h.

Discussion

How are the sounds different? What parts of their body touched the floor when they were the butterfly/caterpillar – whole foot, ball of the foot, hands, fingers, trunk, knees? Which did they like being the best?

Follow-up activities

✧ Explore moving like worms, spiders and snails.
✧ Use music and make up a dance involving three different insects.

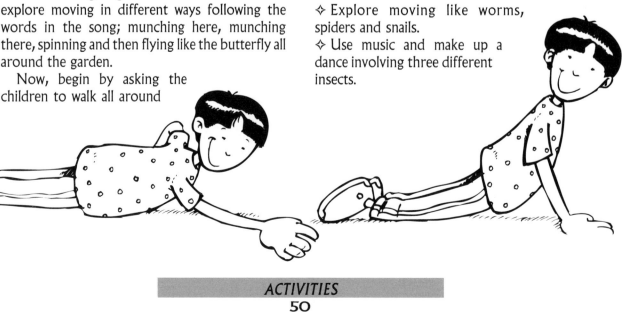

CHAPTER 6
ALL KINDS OF INSECTS

Investigate a range of minibeasts in this chapter by drawing an ant map, learning a bee dance and looking under stones to see what lurks there!

WHO AM I?

Objective

English – To practise asking questions to develop speaking and listening skills.

Group size

Pairs.

What you need

Pieces of card, pencils, a list of questions and clues, knowledge of minibeasts (used at the beginning and end of topic to assess knowledge and understanding). A collection of minibeast pictures (for pre-readers).

Preparation

Make a set of 'minibeast guessing cards' by writing three clues about each different type of minibeast onto separate pieces of card and finishing with the question, 'Who am I?'. An example could be: I am black, I have eight legs, I cannot fly – Who am I? Make picture cards for pre-readers.

What to do

Ask the children to get into pairs and explain that one person in the pair must read out the clues and ask the question 'Who am I?' and the other must try and guess which minibeast is being described.

Choose one child to demonstrate the game with you. Explain that if they cannot guess the minibeast from the clues then they should try and think of some questions to ask. Give them some ideas for asking questions, such as: What colour is it? How many legs has it got? and so on.

If the child cannot guess after hearing the three clues and asking some questions, try the next card. After five minutes ask the pairs to swap over. Count how many each child managed to guess.

Discussion

Which minibeast is being described? What clue gave it away? Which minibeast is the easiest to guess and why? What colour is the most popular when describing minibeasts? What do you do if you are not sure how to answer?

Follow-up activities

✧ Ask the children to make up their own cards and try them out at home or with some friends.
✧ Paint some 'fantasy' minibeasts and give them new names.
✧ Find the minibeasts on the word search on photocopiable page 94.
✧ Choose one minibeast and ask everyone to find out an interesting fact about it.

UNDER A STONE

. . . .

Objective

Science — To investigate and explore life under a stone, recognising and classifying insects.

Group size

Whole group or small group.

What you need

An outside area such as a garden or park to visit with stones or logs that can be lifted up to explore the minibeasts life underneath, paper, pencils, a camera, bug containers.

Preparation

The children need to know quite clearly what they are looking for and why they may have to lift up stones to find such creatures. Observe Health and Safety guidelines when undertaking visits, ensuring that the children are well supervised at all times.

What to do

Investigate the chosen site before taking the children there and check under stones and logs to make sure there is an adequate supply of wildlife to observe. Remind the children of safety before you go out in your group.

On your visit organise the children in small groups with an adult. When they find any minibeasts remind them to handle them carefully and collect them and place them in the appropriate collecting jar. Bring the jars back to look at later.

Ask the children to remember which stones they found their minibeasts under. Draw a plan to identify the stones and log, giving each a special name to help the children recall. Return the minibeasts where you found them as soon as possible. Place the stone or log back in exactly the same position.

Visit the same stones or logs every so often to see if different insects come and go. Record what has been found under the logs or stones by drawing pictures or making a list.

Discussion

Where were insects found? What were they doing? How many did you find? Do you know all the names of the minibeasts/insects? How could you find out? Looking another time, did you find the same/different minibeasts?

Follow-up activities

✧ Make a small minibeasts environment in the sand tray; replace the sand with soil and large stones and visit it each day. Are there any insects?
✧ Paint a picture of a minibeast on a stone then varnish it to make a paper weight.
✧ Keep a diary/notebook to record what minibeasts have been seen.
✧ Use photocopiable page 95 to keep a survey of all minibeasts found; tick the chart when you have found some minibeasts in each location.

WHO LIVES IN MY GARDEN?

Objective

Art – To construct hand-painted masks for role-play.

Group size

Up to six children.

What you need

Pictures of minibeasts, card, elastic, hole punch, felt-tipped pens/paintbrushes, pencil, scissors, collage materials.

Preparation

Measure each child's face and cut out or ask the children to cut out the base template for a mask. Look and talk about minibeasts and their facial characteristics. Put out the resources to encourage and inspire the children to make minibeast masks.

What to do

Ask the children to each choose which minibeast to represent on their masks. Ask them to look at pictures (or the real thing) and consider the shape of the minibeast.

Cut out the appropriate shape on each child's mask template, and consider the characteristics of the minibeast. Let the children choose to put in specific details using paint, felt-tipped pens or the collage materials.

Once the masks are complete allow the children to play in small groups role-playing their chosen minibeasts.

Provide a suitable environment for the children to play, with green material for the ground and logs and large pebbles.

Discussion

Where do you live? What kind of things have you got in your home? What do you eat? Do you move quickly or slowly? Do you fly or crawl? Do you make any noises? Do you have any enemies who may eat you?

Follow-up activities

✧ Display the masks on the wall and write a fact file caption for each one.
✧ Place small plastic insects in boxes to create a 'minibeast museum'.
✧ Make up a short play involving three of the children as minibeasts.

BEASTIE LINE

Objective

Mathematics – To create a number counting line.

Group size

Ten children.

What you need

Plastic insects (available from educational suppliers), A4 coloured card, felt-tipped pens, adhesive, access to a photocopier, scissors, Blu-Tack.

Preparation

Check that the insects photocopy well, and copy several of each type on each sheet of paper.

What to do

Ask each child to clearly write a number on a piece of card (each choosing a different one up to ten). Hand out the sheets of photocopied insects and let the children choose which insect they are going to 'collect'. Now, ask them to cut out the correct amount of their insect to match the number on their card. Check that they each have the correct number and then let them glue the insects in place.

Put some Blu-Tack on the cards as they are completed and display them in sequence on the wall in order to form a line of one to ten. Use your minibeast number line for any number work or counting activities. Remember to check that the numbers are correctly formed and support those children who need help.

Discussion

What comes before three? What comes after? How many minibeasts are on your card? Count and check how many minibeasts are on the next sheet to yours. Can you write every number correctly? Are there more spiders than ladybirds? How many legs are on some of the minibeasts?

Follow-up activities

✧ Make a 3D number line up to five; put out five numbered boxes or trays and on each one place the correct amount of minibeasts.
✧ Make a number line using all spiders, or ladybirds, and make it go up to ten putting the minibeasts in different patterns than in the original mixed minibeasts line.
✧ Draw a chalk number line outside.

ROGUE'S GALLERY

Objective

RE – To learn to treat all living things with care and concern.

Group size

Up to six children.

What you need

Small cake tins (one between two children), sets of plastic replica insects, card, felt markers, reference books about insects, a collection of small stones, twigs, pieces of wood, bark, flowers, some earth and sand.

Preparation

Put some earth/sand in the tins. Have all the materials to hand. Make name labels to go with each insect.

What to do

Explain to the children they will be making up pretend homes for the different insects. Show an insect and talk about it, ask has it got wings, feelers or a mouth? Let the children tell you what each insect needs. They may suggest the sort of things they use themselves such as TVs and duvets! Accept their suggestions but encourage them to use the reference books to find out more.

Emphasise that real insects are not to be played with, they are living things and that many are useful to us. Let the children work in pairs with their 'cake tin homes', choosing one of the insects and deciding all the things it needs, taking good care of it and providing for its food and protection.

When they have finished furnishing the 'homes' put them all on display.

Discussion

Ask the children to tell you about the differences between the insects: How does your insect move? Does it have legs or wings? Where does it like to live – in the ground, on the ground, in the air? What does it eat? Do they all need the same things? Discuss what is harmful for the insect. (Us, predators, insecticides.) What would happen if they were destroyed?

Follow-up activities

✧ Make a scrap book containing 'amazing facts' about insects: how big, how strong, how many, how they can carry heavy loads and so on.
✧ Make sets of 'insects' and 'not insects', find out what decides if a creature is an insect or not. (All insects have three parts to their bodies, antennae, most have large eyes, all insects have three pairs of jointed legs (although some do not have these all their lives), most insects have wings. Spiders are not insects.)
✧ Keep a notebook of places and types of insects you have seen.

ANT CITY

Objective

Geography – To make simple maps and use directions.

Group size

Up to six children.

What you need

Large sheet of backing paper, black sugar paper, coloured paper for scenery or features, scissors, adhesive, card and felt-tipped pens, Blu-Tack, live ants for observation.

Preparation

Prepare the card to make labels for the map saying – left, right, up, down, under, inside, outside, over. Leave some card blank for any special features of the ants' journey and fill in later. Look for black ants in nests under large flat stones, between paving stones or on rose bushes, yellow ants prefer to live in grass. Always carefully replace stones once you have looked under them. Encourage ants by leaving out ripe fruit, seeds or a blob of jam.

What to do

Ants live in a colony, so if you find one you know there will be others nearby. Forager ants (without wings) leave the colony to find food. Be aware that some ants can sting.

Take a small group of children outside to observe the ants. Watch them for a while and you may even see them playing games together; they even pretend to fight but do not shoot out their poison at each other as they would an enemy. Place an obstacle in the path of the ants and observe what happens. If you find the entrance to the colony see if you can tell which ants are guarding the entrance, these are sentries who stop any enemies getting in. Observe how they are able to carry heavy or large objects.

Back inside, let the children use the backing paper and the black sugar paper to make an 'ant map', ask them to show which direction the ants travel in and how they get over or around any obstacles in their path. Place the labels on the map and mark any features such as 'big stone' or 'pine needles'. Talk through the ants' journey with the whole group.

Discussion

What do you think the ants are doing? They all have important duties and work very hard for the colony. Are the ants all going in the same direction? Where do you think they are going? Are they carrying anything? Could you carry something that was heavier or bigger than yourself? Where do they like to live? (They live in social colonies in nests, in tunnels underground and come to the surface for food.) How do they know where to go and what to do? (Ants are able to pass on messages through an ant kiss. They stand up on two legs and pass a liquid into each others mouths. They also stroke and tap each others antennae.)

Follow-up activities

✧ Make a simple map of the route to your setting; draw pictures to show any special or favourite features on the way.
✧ Learn the song 'Five little ants' page 82 and the poem 'The ants' tea party' page 72.
✧ Using a similar format to *We're going on a bear hunt* Michael Rosen (Walker Books), make up a poem about a forager ant going looking for food.

GIANT FOOTSTEPS

Objective

Mathematics – To compare sizes and to use non-standard measurement.

Group size

Four to six children.

What you need

A4 paper for each child, colouring pencils, scissors, adhesive, card, a collection of plastic insects.

Preparation

Draw around one of the children's shoes to make a template.

What to do

Show the children the shoe shape you have cut out and ask them to imagine the shoe is walking in the garden and to consider how many insects the foot in the shoe might walk over as it makes its way across the garden.

Take the shoe shape and the plastic insects and ask the children to guess how many insects will fit onto the shoe. Sort the insects by size, the smallest to the largest. Let the children select one size and cover the shoe shape with them, encourage them to count how many insects were needed.

Use the same idea to make a card: show the children how to fold a piece of paper into four to form a greeting card shape, open it out and draw a garden scene with lots of insects, butterflies and bees. Fold the top to the bottom to recreate the greeting card centre spread and on the right hand side draw a large shoe, cut almost all the way around the foot shape to form a flap. Lift up to see what lies underneath your shoe!

Discussion

What sort of things do you walk over in the garden? What would you look like to a snail or a spider? What is it like to be too big or too small to do something? When does it matter? When the children cover the shoe shape does the size of the insect make a difference to the number counted?

Follow-up activities

✧ Mathematical insects – look at number patterns, the number of legs, wings, different shapes and sizes of bodies.
✧ Read stories that use different sizes as a crucial part of the plot, such as 'Jack and the Beanstalk', 'Three Billy Goats Gruff', (Traditional) or *The BFG* by Roald Dahl (Jonathan Cape).
✧ Make a giant ladybird, butterfly or snail for a minibeasts display.
✧ Arrange other things in order of size: teddies, dolls, cups or mugs.

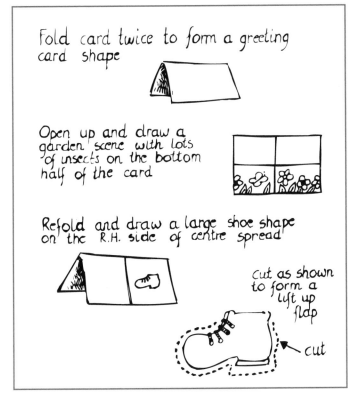

Fold card twice to form a greeting card shape

Open up and draw a garden scene with lots of insects on the bottom half of the card

Refold and draw a large shoe shape on the R.H. side of centre spread

Cut as shown to form a lift up flap

cut

BEE DANCE

Objective

PE – To learn a sequence of movements.

Group size

Whole group if sufficient space.

What you need

A space to move around in freely, card, pens, music (optional).

Preparation

The children should be comfortably dressed or change into loose clothing so that they can move freely, they should wear plimsolls or have bare feet. Use the card to make labels or symbols; one set of cards should show a larger flower (or the letter N to represent nectar), provide one nectar card for each group of three to four children. One large card should show the sun. Place the cards face-up on the floor around the room.

What to do

Explain that a worker bee leaves the hive to find nectar (this is the sweet juice of the flowers). The worker sucks in the nectar through its long tongue and into the honey bag where it turns into honey, and then carries it back to the hive. When a bee has found a good source of nectar it will return to the hive to tell the others. Worker bees go and search for food for many miles from the hive, they need lots of nectar to feed the growing larvae and they need help to bring it back. Bees are able to communicate with each other through a sequence of movements.

Explain to the children that they are going to pretend to be the bees who have found some delicious nectar and need to send a message to the rest of the hive to tell them where it is.

Show the children the cards and explain what they represent. In groups of three or four let the children decide secretly which 'N' card is their nectar. They must make up a code or sequence of movements to show how to get to it, just like the worker bees do. For instance they could turn around and wave their arms to represent the sun and then indicate with different body movements where to go next. Start with a simple sequence of three different movements.

Let each group show their dance. Can the rest of the group understand it and guess which nectar card they have chosen?

Discussion

Ask the children what was their favourite part, dancing or making up the code? Why do the bees need to have a special code? Can they think of other ways the bees could give out their message?

Follow-up activities

✧ Look at other signs and symbols to communicate – road signs, advertisements or warnings.
✧ Work with simple routes and maps, draw lines to show a journey. Make a group map showing the route the bees took from the hive to the flower.
✧ Use grids as treasure maps with compass points, north, south, east, west. Give children directions to follow; four steps south, now two steps north.

CHAPTER 7
DISPLAYS

IDEAS FOR DISPLAY

Whenever you are making a display consider who it is for and why you are setting up the display. You may be making a display as a starting point to an activity to create an interest and as a stimulus to the children. Alternatively you may be making a display at the end of your project to pull all the work on a particular theme together as an end result. Either way the display is bound to provide an attractive focal point which will create a certain atmosphere and encourage discussion. Displaying the children's work also gives them the message that you value what they have created.

Your displays will be for the children themselves, their parents and other visitors to your group. If your intention is that the children will use the display and interact with it, make sure it is accessible to them and at the appropriate height. This kind of display may not look perfect all the time as it is a working display.

A good display may invite questions and comments, present the familiar in an unusual way and remember that once a display has 'become part of the wallpaper' it's time to make a change.

Setting up

You may find it useful to keep a set of tools in a tool box. Include a good stapler, craft knife, wallpaper edging tool, pins, long-necked drawing pins, Velcro, light hammer, cup hooks and screws.

When fixing up backing paper you may discover that your walls are not straight. To pin up vertically you may need to make a plumb line with a piece of string and a weight at the bottom (a drawing pin or a blob of Plasticine). To achieve a straight line horizontally measure the distance from the top edge at each side, push in pins to mark and attach a length of cotton as a guide. Once your paper is in place remove the pins and cotton.

Corrugated paper / card will stand up on its own and provide a good background for a display. Fabric, or pieces of sheeting are useful especially if your surface is old and damaged.

Always aim for variety with your displays, positioning items at different levels to take the eye to the focal point. Try using boxes with lengths of fabric draped over them to make levels.

UNDERGROUND WORM NEST

This display is based on the activities in Chapter 3 'Worms'.

Display content

The children's worm shaped sock puppets (page 28).
Spaghetti and brown wool glued to the background paper as wiggly worms.
Children's observational drawings (see Follow up activity page 32) of real worms, double mounted on beige and brown paper.
Children's concertina books about worms (see Follow-up activity on page 29).
Reference books displayed on book stands.
Leaf shapes cut from sugar paper.

Colours and textures

Use browns and creams as a colour scheme. Suspend a large sheet of paper (50cm) in front of the display with observational holes to view the life in a worm nest behind. Use cup hooks or screws for fixing items from the ceiling. To represent earth use a flour and water

mixture, cooked for a few minutes and mixed with brown paint. Use dark red and orange leaves.

Decorative border

Make a border using a finger dipped in paint to indicate a worm trail.

Label suggestions

Use folded card so that the labels will stand up. Write out the poem 'A tiny, tiny worm' (page 74). Use worm shapes for lettering. Ask questions such as: How many worms can you see? Which is the longest worm?

A SUMMER MEADOW

This display is based on the activities in Chapter 6 'All kinds of insects'.

Display contents

Any pictures and drawings of minibeasts and insects which the children have made.
Booklets of the children's writing.
Lift-up stone shapes with insect drawings underneath.
The children's minibeast masks (page 53) displayed in the front.
Plastic insects exhibition with appropriate name tags for each type.

Colours and textures

Bright summery colours. Pale blue background as the summer sky. Long green grasses and flowers made from tissue paper and Cellophane.

Variety of textures for the insects and the minibeasts. Attach some of the creatures onto small boxes so that they stand away from the background. Suspend others so that they will move in the breeze.

Display the plastic insect exhibition on a low table in front of the meadow scene.

Decorative border

Print insect shapes around the edge of the display area using shapes cut out from a sponge dipped in black paint.

Label suggestions

Use Who am I? questions, such as: Which insect is in the air, on the leaf or under a stone?
Make a questionnaire for the children to complete in pairs. Ask: How many bees are in the garden? How many minibeasts live under a stone?

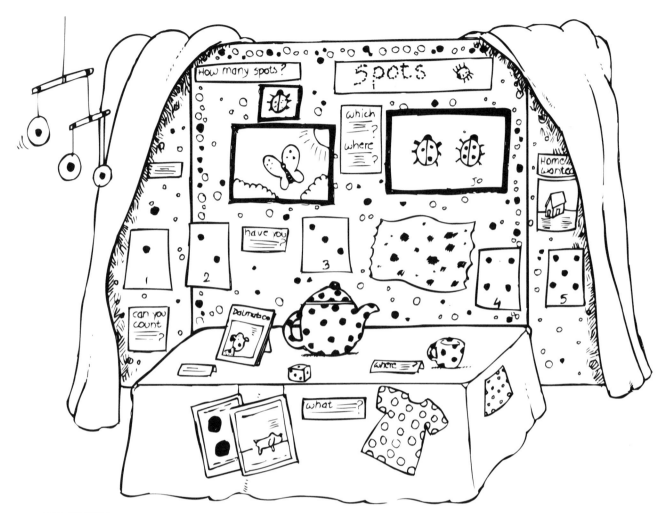

SPOTS

. . . .

This display is linked to the activities in Chapter 1 'Ladybirds'.

Display content

Children's ladybird books (page 12).
Ladybird number line (page 11).
Home wanted! adverts (page 18).
Pictures of ladybirds, butterflies or other insects with spotted markings.
Mugs, plates and other household items with spots on.
Wrapping paper, fabric with spots.
Story books about spots such as any 'Spot the dog' books by Eric Hill (Heinemann).
Tissue paper circles, sticky paper circles.

Colour and textures

Cover the display board with spotted paper (either bought wrapping paper or print spots onto a plain sheet of sugar paper). Pleat a drape at the side or centre if necessary, depending on the number of items you will be including in the display. Make the main label 'Spots' using dots.

From the ceiling hang mobiles made from card circles. Place all the spotted items where the children can touch and examine them. Use the display to encourage counting by making a number line with spots to count. Add a dice to the display.

Decorative border

Make a border using dots on thin strips of paper stapled around the edge of the display board.

Label suggestions

Can you count the spots? Which animals / minibeasts have spots? (Ladybirds, certain dogs, cheetahs.) Have you got any spots? Do you have any spotty clothes? What kinds of dogs have spots? How many spots has a ladybird got?

SPIRALS

● ●

This display is linked to the activity 'Round and round' (page 22) in Chapter 2 'Snails'.

Display contents

Children's clay snails (page 22).
String and skipping ropes made into spiral shapes.
Large springs and screws.
Plants with spiralling creeping patterns.
Shells with spiral patterns on.
Circles cut in spirals, suspended.

Colours and textures

Use a sheet of backing paper which the children have printed with spiral shapes. Alternatively stick up lengths of string glued into coils to give a 3D background effect.

Decorative border

Use a single strip of plain paper to provide a simple border in order not to detract from the main focus of the display.

Label suggestions

Spirals go round and round. Spirals go up and down. Can you find any more spirals? Can you make a spiral? What happens when you go down a helter skelter or a 'tube' at the swimming pool? Do the spirals make you go faster or slower?

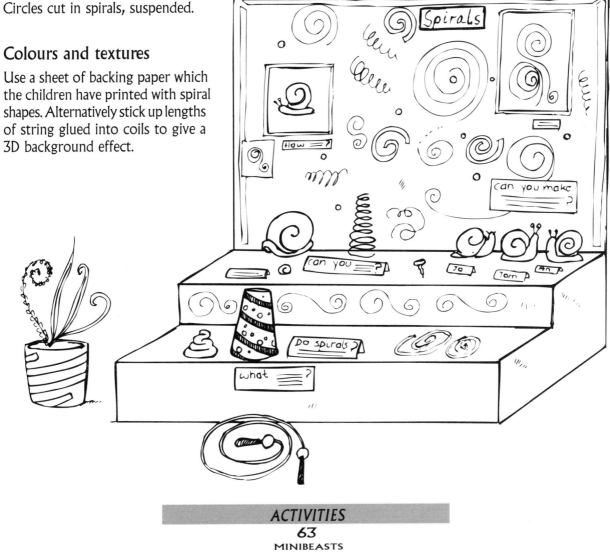

CHAPTER 8
ASSEMBLIES

In this chapter you will find ideas for assemblies about honey bees, spiders, caterpillars and butterflies. An activity, reflection, prayer and song are suggested for each theme.

THE HONEY BEE

Resources

A selection of different types of honey, perhaps spread onto small pieces of bread. Other products (edible and otherwise) which contain honey.

Introduction

Remind the children of any work they have done based on the theme of the honey bee. Ask the children to show pictures and models which they have created and encourage them to review appropriate stories, sing relevant songs and recite poems or rhymes which they have learned.

Activity

Invite some of the children to present a short drama or role-play about the way in which bees produce honey.

Choose some other children to come and taste some of the different kinds of honey and products containing honey, which form your display. Ask the children to think of different words to describe the taste of honey (good, lovely, sweet, sticky) and write these on a flip chart or an OHP transparency.

Reflection

Slowly read out the words which you have recorded, and ask the children to think about all the sweet, good, lovely things, moments or people that they have experienced in their own lives. In a small group or gathering, some children might be willing to share their thoughts with others.

Prayer

Some children might like to join in a prayer which celebrates all that is good and lovely. This could be composed by the children themselves or might be prepared by the adult.

Remind the children that bees spread pollen to ensure that trees and other plants will bear good fruit. Invite the children to consider ways in which they might be able to spread goodness in the world around them and devise a prayer which asks for God's help in this undertaking.

Music

The Corrymela Community has produced a song called *The Pollen of Peace* which is featured in Christianity Topic Book 3 by Margaret Cooling (RMEP) which would be appropriate for this assembly.

As the children prepare to leave the assembly area you could play a recording of Rimsky Korsakov's *Flight of the Bumble Bee*.

THE PROPHET MUHAMMED AND THE SPIDER

Resources

A large ball of string/twine.
Recording of 'the call to prayer' (optional).

Introduction

Play a recording of the 'call to prayer' as the children enter the assembly area, if possible.

Remind the children of any work which has been based on the life cycles of various minibeasts (page 43) emphasising the ways in which different species depend on one another. Invite the children to show pictures or models, or to present short role-plays depicting these life cycles.

Activity

Tell the children the story of The Prophet Muhammed and the Spider (below).

Many, many years ago, there lived a man called the Prophet Muhammed. He worked in the city of Makkah and he was extremely clever and wise. He told the people who lived in the city that they should worship only one God, but some of the people were very angry with him. They wanted to worship lots of different Gods and so they did not like what Muhammed was saying.

Eventually, Muhammed decided to leave Makkah and escape from all those who opposed him. Armed men came to his house to try to kill him, but they did not find him there – he had already disappeared into the mountains. His enemies offered a huge reward to anyone who could capture him, but Muhammed and his friends found safety in a cave.

While they were still in the cave, friends brought them food and drink, but they were still aware that they might be discovered. The Prophet Muhammed's enemies were still searching everywhere for him and they wondered if he might be hiding in a secret place.

The Prophet Muhammed was protected in his cave by different animals; a spider spun a huge web over the entrance to the cave and some doves built a nest there. The Prophet's enemies eventually found the cave, saw the web and the nest and thought that the cave must have been empty for

many years, so they began to search elsewhere! The Prophet Muhammed and his friends were safe.

Muslim people today believe that the Prophet was a very special person and that God sent the spider and the doves to help protect him from his enemies.

Involve the children in presenting the story by encouraging them to show the other children their illustrations of the key events or by enabling them to act out parts of it using appropriate costumes and props.

It is vital to remember that Muslims consider it disrespectful to depict God, the Prophet Muhammed or any of the other Prophets in any way, shape or form. Pictures and role-play will therefore need to be carefully monitored.

Reflection

Invite some of the children to sit in a circle in the centre of the assembly area. Give one child a ball of string or twine, ask the child to hold onto the end of it, and to pass the ball across the circle to a friend. Invite the children to pass it back and forth across the circle until a web-like effect has been created.

If possible carry this out without the children making a sound and with appropriate music playing in the background. A recording of a piano piece by Erik Satie would be suitable, as his work generally has a slow, measured pace.

Prayer

Display pictures, posters, slides or OHP transparencies which show the intricacy of a spider's web. Some children might like to join in a prayer (either out loud or in silence) which explores two relevant themes:
• the tenacity and skill of a small spider;
• the way in which the Prophet was helped by a seemingly insignificant creature.

This could be composed by the children themselves or might be prepared by the teacher.

Music

As the children prepare to leave the assembly area, some of them might like to join in a relevant song such as 'Spiders' on page 87.

Otherwise you could play a recording of a Qur'anic recitation if available.

FROM A CATERPILLAR TO A BUTTERFLY

Resources

The Very Hungry Caterpillar by Eric Carle (Hamish Hamilton), ideally in a 'big book' format or presented as story boards.

Introduction

Remind the children of any work the may have done based on the life cycle of the caterpillar/butterfly (page 43). Show slides or OHP transparencies which mark the different stages of development or invite some children to display their own pictures or models based on this theme.

Activity

Read or tell the story of *The Very Hungry Caterpillar* placing particular emphasis on the great change from small, fat, green caterpillar to brightly coloured, flying butterfly.

Involve the children in presenting the story by encouraging them to show their own illustrations of the key events or by enabling them to act it out, using appropriate costumes and props.

Reflection

Display the children's pictures or models which illustrate change from one state into another:
• caterpillar – butterfly;
• tadpole – frog;
• seed/bulb – flower;
• bare twig – twig covered with leaves or blossom;
• egg – chick;
• death – life (with particular emphasis on the Easter story).

Play a recording of some calm, peaceful music, such as Debussy's *L'Apres Midi d'une Faune* and invite the children to spend a few quiet moments reflecting on the changes taking place around them in the natural world.

Some children could be asked to depict the metamorphosis from caterpillar to butterfly through movement and dance, using the chosen music as an accompaniment.

Consider holding this assembly in the open air so that the theme of this reflection is self-evident in the actual surroundings.

Prayer

Display pictures, posters or slides which show the beauty of butterflies and other minibeasts. Some children might then like to join in a prayer (either out loud or in silence) which highlights the loveliness of creation, especially in spring time.

This could be a prayer of thanks devised by the children themselves or by an adult:
We thank you God
For the beauty of this time of year
And for reminding us
That in the darkness
New life is waiting to emerge.
Amen

As an alternative use a poem – such as Gerard Manley Hopkins' *Glory be to God for Dappled Things* – as a prayer.

Music

As the children prepare to leave the assembly area, some of them might like to join in a hymn, such as 'If I Were a Butterfly, I'd Thank You Lord for Giving me Wings' or 'Caterpillar Munch' from page 83 of this book.

Collective Worship in Schools

The assemblies outlined here are suitable for use with children in nurseries and playgroups, but would need to be adapted for use with pupils at registered schools. As a result of legislation enacted in 1944, 1988 and 1993, there are now specific points to be observed when developing a programme of Collective Acts of Worship in a school.

Further guidance will be available from your local SACRE – Standing Advisory Council for RE.

POEMS AND ACTION RHYMES

LADY DOT!

I'm a one-spot
two-spot
ladybird.
A dot-to-dot
a helicopter
lady-bird.

Flapping in the rose bush,
flipping to the sky:
a helicopter,
dot-to-dot,
come and count
each shining spot,
lady-bird
LET'S FLY!

Judith Nicholls

BELLYFOOT✢

[✢literal translation of gastropod]

Bellyfoot
Bellyfoot
Squidgy
Squeezy
Jellyfoot
Stretchy
Squashy
Slider,
Soft and
Slimy
Glider.
Bellyfoot
No-leg
No-toe
No-nail,
Bellyfoot
Never
Needs a
Wellyfoot –
Snail!

Sue Cowling

THERE'S A SPIDER IN MY BATH!

I can't see his web,
I can't see any flies.
I wonder what he eats all day
to make him such a size?

I can't see his mouth,
I can't see his eyes.
I wonder *how* he eats each day
to make him such a size?

Judith Nicholls

PHOTOCOPIABLE RESOURCES

HOW TO MAKE A BUTTERFLY

Take a sheet of paper,
Blob the colours you like best,
Fold it in the middle
Like a butterfly at rest.

Open up the paper
That you painted jewel-bright.
When its wings have dried
You'll see a butterfly in flight!

Sue Cowling

UNDER A STONE...

Under a stone where the earth was firm,
(one forefinger for the worm)
I found a wriggly, wriggly worm;
(cover it with other hand)
'Good morning,' I said.

'How are you today?'
(uncover finger)
But the wriggly worm
just wriggled away!
(wriggle other forefinger along other arm)

THIS IS LITTLE TIMOTHY SNAIL...

This is little Timothy Snail,
(Clench right fist with thumb sticking out)
His house on his back.

One day two men came along,
And popped him in a sack.
(Right hand covered by left hand)

At last he managed to get out,
(Right hand creeps out of left hand)
Out of a hole so small.

What became of him after that
(Right hand goes out of sight)
I've never been told at all.
(Shake head slowly)

SNAIL

A snail
makes hardly any
noise.
He creeps
upon
his way
and only moves
an inch or two
with not a word
to say.

His tiny eyes
come out on stalks
and tell him
what's around.
He leaves a smooth
and silver track
behind him
on the ground.

Jean Kenward

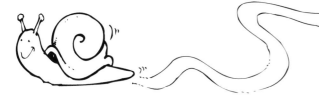

JOIN THE QUEUE

From the middle of my apple
cried a wiggly worm
'I was here first
so please wait your turn!'

This can also be a shape poem:

From
   the
     middle
   of
   my
   apple
    cried
      a
       wiggly
      worm
   'I
  was
here
first
 so
   please
     wait
   your
turn!'

John Walsh

THE EARTHWORM

In everybody's flower bed I always can be
found.
I mix up all the stones and soil as I move
underground.
I'm long and slim and slimy and I slither
under logs.
I'd make a tasty dinner for the hedgehogs,
birds and frogs!
But if you hold me in your hand I'll
squiggle and I'll squirm.
I have no arms and legs because I am a
wriggly worm.

Jill Atkins

LITTLE SPIDER

Spider, spider, little spider,
hanging from a thread.
I can see you as I'm lying
snugly in my bed.
Spider, spider, little spider,
don't come down I beg.
I really couldn't bear it
if you landed on my head.

Jan Pollard

SPIDERY-SPY

What are you making
my soft-spinning spider?
What are you building,
spidery-spy?

*I'm spinning a silk net
to hunt for my breakfast,
a fine web to dine on
and catch me a fly.*

What will you do then,
my spidery-spinner?
Where will you go to,
spidery-spoo?

*I'll lie here in wait
for a plump young mosquito
to eat for my supper
as all spiders do.*

Where will you sleep then,
My spidery-hunter?
What will you dream of,
spidery-spee?

*I'll swing in my hammock
and dream of my spiderlings;
here in the moonlight,
that's where I'll be.*

Judith Nicholls

CHRYSALIS

One little chrysalis lived on a twig
Full of food to make him big
Popped one day as I passed by
Turned into a butterfly!

Maureen Warner

INCY WINCY SPIDER

Incy Wincy spider
Climbing up the spout;
Down came the rain
And washed the spider out:
Out came the sun
And dried up all the rain;
Incy Wincy spider
Climbing up again.

Anon

LADYBIRD, LADYBIRD

Ladybird, ladybird
Fly away home!
Your house is on fire
And your children all gone;
All except one
And that's little Ann
And she has crept under
The warming pan.

Anonymous

LITTLE CATERPILLAR

Here's a little caterpillar
{waggle index finger}
looking for her tea.
She nibbles at a bean
{nibble index finger on other hand}
and she nibbles at a pea.
(nibble finger + thumb circle)
She nibbles at a peach
(nibble finger of fist)
and she nibbles at a plum.
(nibble finger + thumb circle)
Then she falls fast asleep
with a nice full tum.
(lay finger on open palm)
Here's a little caterpillar
opening her eyes.
(wiggle index finger awake on palm)
Look! She's grown a pair of wings
(link open palms with thumbs)
Up and up she flies.
(fly hand upward and away)

Tony Mitton

LITTLE ARABELLA MILLER

Little Arabella Miller
Found a woolly caterpillar.
First it crawled upon her mother,
Then upon her baby brother;
All said, 'Arabella Miller,
Take away this caterpillar!'

Anonymous

THE ANTS' TEA PARTY

The ants came marching,
one by one.
They nibbled at the biscuits
and the big, round bun.

The ants came marching
two by two.
They trampled in the jam
till their legs turned blue.

The ants came marching,
three by three.
They gobbled up the sugar
and they drank up the tea.

The ants came marching,
four by four.
They finished off the crumbs,
then they marched out the door.

Tony Mitton

I WISH I WAS A LITTLE GRUB

I wish I was a little grub
With whiskers on my tummy,
I'd climb into a honey-pot
And make my tummy gummy.

Anonymous

PHOTOCOPIABLE RESOURCES

LADYBIRD, LADYBIRD

Ladybird, ladybird
don't fly away.
Live in my garden,
I want you to stay.

I've little green bugs
all over my trees.
Some come back and eat them
ladybird, please.

Tony Mitton

THE SPIDER'S TEA

*Hold one hand up and open with fingers stretched
out to suggest a spider's web. Walk, fly or hop each
minibeast into the web in cue with the words.*

In went the beetle.
(Stumble hand across into web)
In went the fly.
(Fly hand across and stick it to web)
In went the bug
(Stumble hand across into web)
with the googly eye
(Then make circle around eye with index finger and
thumb on 'googly eye')
In went the ant.
(Stumble hand across as with beetle)
(Ppptt!) In went the flea.
(Leap flea across into web with quick splat sound)
'Ah!' said the spider.
'Here's my tea!'
(Waggle hand in air, scuttle eagerly towards net)

Tony Mitton

MINIATURE WORLD

There's place in the playground,
round at the back,
where the weeds grow out
of a tiny crack.

There are knobbly pebbles,
twigs and dust,
and a patch of fence
that's nibbled with rust.

If you lift a leaf
or disturb a stone
you may see a beetle
stumbling alone.

It's a miniature world
for anyone to see.
But nobody's noticed it.
Only me.

Tony Mitton

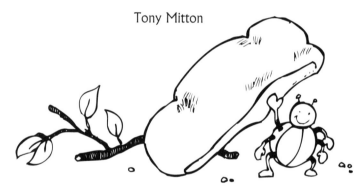

MINIBEAST MOODS

I wonder how the snail feels
underneath its shell?
Is it happy?
Is it sad?
It's very hard to tell.

I wonder how the slug feels
as it slides along.
I wonder if it wants to sing
a slow and slimy song?

I wonder how the worm feels
sifting through the soil?
Is it grumpy?
Is it bored
with all its weary toil?

I wonder how the louse feels
rolled up in a ball?

It's hard to know
because they don't
say anything at all.

Tony Mitton

A TINY, TINY WORM

A tiny, tiny worm
Wriggled along the ground;
It wriggled along like this
Without a sound.

It came to a tiny hole,
A tiny hole in the ground,
It wriggled right inside
Without a sound.

Wyn Daniel Evans

STORIES

CREEPY CRAWLY CATERPILLAR

When the word was new, Creepy Crawly Caterpillar lived in a bright new forest. Sometimes he went for a creep-crawl but mostly he didn't bother. He just lay on a leaf in the sun, dreamily looking around him.

His friend, Worker Ant, also lived in the forest. Ant liked to be busy. Busy! busy! busy! Gathering food for the ant hill.

'Please, stop and chat!' Creepy Crawly Caterpillar said one day.

'I can't stop long. I'm busy! busy! busy!' Ant replied.

Suddenly they saw a bee go by. Swoop! swoop! swoop! from flower to flower.

'I wish I could do that,' Creepy Crawly Caterpillar said.

Ant laughed. 'You can't swoop! You're a creepy crawly like me. Your feet belong safe on the ground.'

But then they saw a ladybird, whizzing in circles, round and round.

Creepy Crawly Caterpillar clapped and cheered. 'I wish I could do that too,' he sighed. 'And I wish! wish! wish! I could dance on the breeze like that dandelion puff, don't you, Ant?'

Ant shook his head. 'I'm too busy for daydreams,' he said.

But the next day, Creepy Crawly Caterpillar wasn't all of a dream, and he wasn't on yesterday's leaf!

'I'm going to be busy! busy! like you, Ant,' he called down. 'I've decided to learn to fly. Here I go. Watch!'

He jumped.

He flapped his legs fast.

But...PLOP!

Ant didn't know whether to laugh or cry. 'You can't fly! You haven't any wings.'

'I don't care what I've got and what I haven't,' Creepy Crawly Caterpillar said. 'I want to fly. I'll try till I can.'

Now, when Ant came by... 'I can't stop to chat! I'm busy! busy! learning to fly.'

But always the same thing happened, PLOP!

Ant told the other workers what Creepy Crawly Caterpillar was up to. They made fun of him when he tried to fly from the Ant Hill.

'All you can do is plop!' they jeered. 'You can't even hop, never mind fly. You'll soon give up, a lazy lump like you!'

But Creepy Crawly Caterpillar didn't give up.

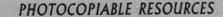

He grew bruised and thin. Ant begged him to stop trying to fly.

'Be your old self again, happy to lie all day in the sun.'

Creepy Crawly Caterpillar began to cry. 'I can't be my old self. I've forgotten how! If I can't fly, nothing else will do. I'll be sad forever.'

He cried so many tears, they wove themselves into a thread.

He hung from the thread so he couldn't see the sky.

But his sorrow grew so great, he couldn't keep it inside. His skin burst, POP!

Ant saw with dismay that the skin beneath was soft and squidgy.

'It won't keep out the rain or the heat of the sun!'

But soon, the soft skin was as hard as stone.

'You've no food in there. Come out!' called Ant. 'You'll starve.'

But Creepy Crawly Caterpillar stayed in his stoney-skin prison day after day, silent and still.

At last, Ant was so worried he fetched the Workers.
'Look!' they said. 'Creepy Crawly Caterpillar's covered in spots! Spots of all colours. What's he trying to be now? A rainbow!' they tittered.

'It's not funny,' said Ant. 'He's sick.'

'He's made himself sick, trying to fly, when he's got sixteen good legs to walk with!'

The Workers hurried off, but Ant stayed with Creepy Crawly Caterpillar. He looked so peculiarly strange, Ant feared that soon his friend would die.

But one sunrise, the stoney prison went CRACK!

It was Creepy Crawly Caterpillar. 'I want to get out. Help, Ant!' he cried.

'Push!' Ant urged. 'Come on, harder.'

At last Creepy Crawly Caterpillar was free. Ant looked at him in surprise. 'You've only got six legs.' Creepy Crawly Caterpillar glanced down. 'And what are these flower-petal things on my sides?'

'I think,' said Ant, 'they could be wings.'

'Wings! Watch, I'll try them!'

Creepy Crawly Caterpillar jumped.

'I didn't plop, Ant. I'm flying! I can fly!

Ant watched in wonder and asked, 'Do I wish I could fly? No,' he said. 'I'm as happy as I am, with my feet where they belong, safe on the ground.'

Off he went, busy! busy! busy! While Creepy Crawly Caterpillar swooped and soared.

That was long ago, but ants are still busy. And caterpillars are still flying.

Kara May

THE HAPPY TREE

Once there was **one** sad and lonely tree who wished very hard for some friends to look after.

One day, **two** big birds saw the lonely tree. They had no home of their own, so they made a big fluffy nest there.

Three spiders saw the lonely tree. They had nowhere to spin their webs, so they hung them from a branch.

Four beautiful butterflies saw the lonely tree. They had been flying all day, so they landed there to rest.

Five curly caterpillars saw the lonely tree. They had nowhere to live, and the tree looked dark and cosy.

Six little ladybirds saw the lonely tree. They were worn out from their journey, so they settled down to sleep.

Seven dizzy daisy seeds saw the lonely tree. They wanted some shade, so they planted themselves nearby — even though the lonely tree had no leaves at all.

When the lonely tree saw all these creatures coming to live with her she began to feel happy. So happy, in fact, that **eight** lush leaves began to grow.

Nine tiny toadstools sprouted in the shelter nearby.

Ten appetising apples hung down from the tree's branches.

So the once lonely tree stood proudly, giving shelter to...

two big birds
three silly spiders
four beautiful butterflies
five curly caterpillars
six little ladybirds
seven dizzy daisies
eight lush leaves
nine tiny toadstools
ten appetising apples
... and was a happy tree ever after!

Joy Cockle

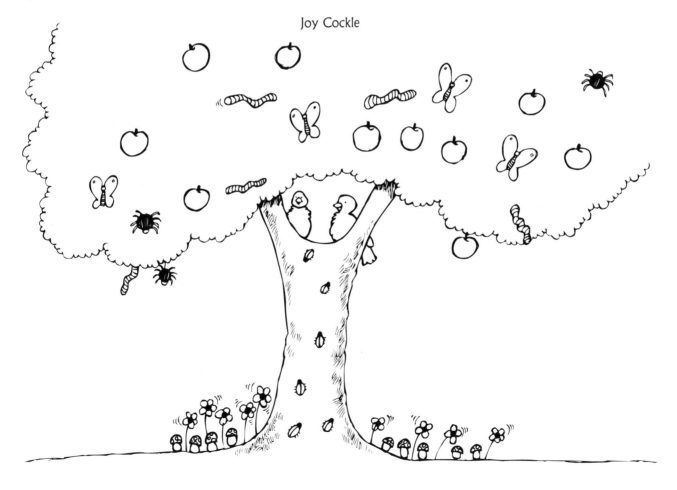

WHO'S THAT IN BEETLE'S HOUSE?

A story from an African folk tale

One day, while Beetle was walking in the forest, a naughty little ant ran into his house. The naughty little ant didn't have a house of his own and he liked Beetle's house so much, he decided to stay.

When he saw Beetle coming home, the naughty little ant stood behind the door and shouted in a big, deep voice: 'DON'T YOU DARE COME IN!'

Beetle stopped, astonished.

'Who's that?' he asked. 'Who's that telling me not to come into my own house?'

The naughty little ant made his voice even bigger: 'I'M A GREAT BIG ANIMAL. I CAN TRAMPLE DOWN ELEPHANTS!'

Beetle was horrified. He hid behind a tree and shivered, wondering what to do.

After a while, Woodlouse came along. He was very concerned to see his friend Beetle so distressed.

'What's the matter, Beetle?' he asked.

'There's someone in my house,' Beetle explained. 'He won't let me in!'

'We'll soon see about that!' said Woodlouse and he marched up to the front door.

'Who's that in Beetle's house?' he called.

The naughty little ant pulled up tall and put on his big deep voice.

'I'M A GREAT BIG ANIMAL,' he shouted. 'I CAN TRAMPLE DOWN ELEPHANTS!'

Woodlouse was horrified. He scuttled straight back to Beetle and stood shivering beside him behind the tree.

After a while, Stick Insect came by and saw them. 'What's the matter?' he asked.

'There's someone in my house,' said Beetle.

'And he won't let us in!' added Woodlouse.

'We'll soon see about that!' said Stick Insect and he marched over to the door. 'Who's that in Beetle house?' he called.

The naughty little ant put on his big deep voice again. 'I'M A GREAT BIG ANIMAL,' he shouted. 'I CAN TRAMPLE DOWN ELEPHANTS!'

PHOTOCOPIABLE RESOURCES

Stick Insect was horrified. He rushed back to Beetle and Woodlouse and hid with them behind the tree.

After a while, Big Hairy Spider came along. 'What's going on?' he asked Beetle.

'There's someone in my house,' said Beetle. 'He won't let me in.'

'We'll soon see about that!' said Hairy Spider.

'Who's that in Beetle's house?' he called, and the naughty little ant replied in his big deep voice. 'I'M A GREAT BIG ANIMAL. I CAN TRAMPLE DOWN ELEPHANTS!'

Big Hairy Spider was horrified. Soon, he too was shivering behind the tree with Beetle, Woodlouse and Stick Insect.

After a while, Little Ladybird came along. 'Goodness gracious!' she said. 'What's the matter with you four?'

'There's someone in my house,' said Beetle.

'He won't let us in,' said Woodlouse.

'He's a great big animal,' added Stick Insect.

'He can trample down elephants!' said Big Hairy Spider.

'Don't be silly,' said Ladybird. 'If he was that big he wouldn't fit into Beetle's house! I'll go and sort it out for you.'

But the naughty little ant heard everything, and as Little Ladybird went in the front door, he ran out at the back. Beetle, Woodlouse, Stick Insect and Big Hairy Spider all crept warily over. 'Well?' they asked. 'Who is in Beetle's house?'

Little Ladybird came out to meet them.

'There's nobody at all in Beetle's house,' she told them. 'It's absolutely empty!'

Sue Palmer

PHOTOCOPIABLE RESOURCES

SPEEDY

It was a damp but sunny morning – the kind Speedy liked best – as he slithered along the garden path, going nowhere in particular. He heard a buzzing noise above his head.

A bee was flying round a flower. 'Buzzz!' said the bee, as it rested on a petal and pushed its head into the centre of the flower to find the nectar.

'Good morning!' called Speedy. 'I'm Speedy!'

The bee almost fell out of the flower. He looked down at Speedy and burst out laughing. 'Speedy! That's a funny name for a *snail!*'

'Why is it?' asked Speedy.

'Well, you don't exactly move fast, do you?' replied the bee. 'You can't zoom through the air like me?'

'Well, no' said Speedy. 'But I can...'

But the bee had already flown off to another flower.

Speedy carried on down the path. He slithered slowly over a large stone and saw a beetle scurrying through the grass.

'Hello, I'm Speedy!' smiled Speedy.

The beetle stopped suddenly, looking round in alarm. The he saw Speedy.

'Oh, you gave me a fright!' he said. Then he started giggling. 'Speedy! Ha! Ha!' He began to roll about in the grass, laughing, and almost turned himself over. 'That's the funniest name for a snail I've heard in a long while. Ha, ha!'

Speedy wasn't very pleased. 'I don't see what's so funny,' he said.

'Well, you're not a fast mover, are you? You can't scurry over the ground like me?'

'Well, no,' agreed Speedy, 'but I can...'

But the beetle had already scurried off, still giggling to himself.

Speedy made his way over to the flower bed, where he munched on a lupin leaf and tried not to feel cross. Suddenly he noted several black ants running around, carrying earth from their nest underground.

'Hello,' called Speedy when one of them ran past him. 'I'm...er...Speedy.'

The ant had run quite a way before he managed to stop, turn round and come back to where Speedy was waiting. He waved his long antennae at the snail, as if trying to work out what he was. Then he made a squeaky, piping noise. 'Hee hee hee hee!' The ant was laughing!

'What's wrong with that! asked Speedy, sharply.

'Fancy calling a *snail* Speedy! squeaked the ant, holding its sides.

'I think it's a nice name,' said Speedy.

'Maybe,' said the ant, gasping for breath, 'but it doesn't suit you, does it? I mean, you can't turn around and tunnel as fast as we can, can you?'

'Maybe not,' said Speedy, 'but I can...'

Suddenly the sky went dark and big drops of rain began to fall.

'Run for cover!' shouted the ant.

'Hurry, it's raining! shouted the beetle.

'Quick! Fly home!' shouted the bee.

They hurried home as fast as they could, but the falling rain was too quick and it soaked them all. Speedy, however, simply tucked himself into his shell where it was nice and dry.

'That's what I've been trying to tell everybody,' his voice echoed from inside his shell. *'I'm called Speedy because I can get into my house quicker than anyone else!'*

Karen King

A FAMOUS SPIDER

Have you ever watched a spider spinning her web? The first thing she has to do is to fasten a line between two branches of the bush where she wants her web to hang, and sometimes this is the most difficult bit. She slides down the line of silk and swings herself backwards and forwards, until she can reach the next branch. Once this line is attached, she can begin to construct her web.

In Scotland, the story goes that when Robert Bruce (who was king of Scotland many years ago) was hiding from his enemies in a shepherd's hut, he was very unhappy. He had lost all his battles with the English king who wanted to take over Scotland, and his wife had been taken prisoner. What was there left for him?

While he was lying on the floor feeling sorry for himself, he noticed a spider trying to make a web in the corner of the roof. Each time she swung her line across to the next beam, she missed. Time and time again she tried to reach the other beam and failed. Robert Bruce wondered why the spider didn't get fed up. But at last she made it. The thread caught and held, so the spider was able to spin her web.

Robert Bruce thought to himself. 'That spider was beaten many times, but she didn't give up. Neither will I!'

So when Spring came, Robert Bruce called his army together. They marched on the English, fought a great battle — and won! Robert's wife came home and once again he was king of Scotland.

Thanks to the patient spider!

Jackie Andrews

SONGS

TONGUE TWISTER

1. Can you wig-gle like a worm? Can you squig-gle? Can you squig-gle like a worm? Can you squirm? Can you wig-gle, wig-gle, squig-gle, squig-gle, squirm, squirm, squirm? Can you wig-gle, squig-gle, squirm like a worm?

2. Can you slither like a snail? Can you quiver?
Can you quiver like a snail? Can you quail?
Can you slither, slither, quiver, quiver, quail, quail, quail?
Can you slither, quiver, quail like a snail?

3. Can you hover like a bee? Can you bumble?
Can you bumble like a bee? Can you buzz?
Can you hover, hover, bumble, bumble, buzz, buzz, buzz?
Can you hover, bumble, buzz like a bee?

Words – Trevor Millum

Music – Gill Parker

FIVE LITTLE ANTS

A counting song which repeats until there are no little ants.

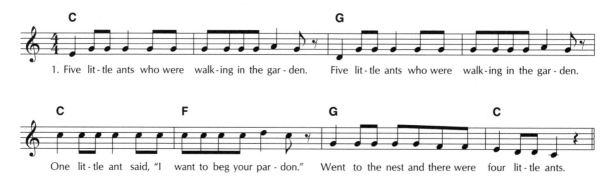

1. Five lit-tle ants who were walk-ing in the gar-den. Five lit-tle ants who were walk-ing in the gar-den. One lit-tle ant said, "I want to beg your par-don." Went to the nest and there were four lit-tle ants.

Clive Barnwell

WORM

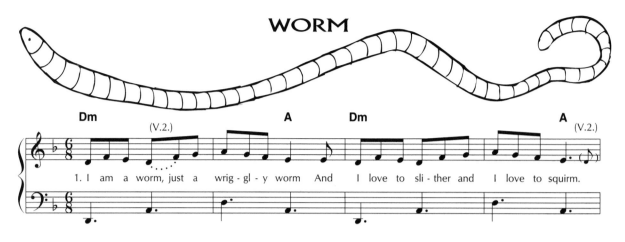

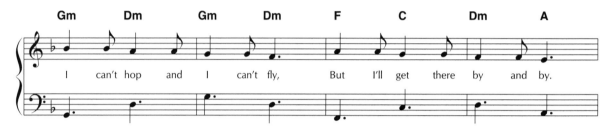

Dm (V.2.) **A** **Dm** **A** (V.2.)

1. I am a worm, just a wrig-gl-y worm And I love to sli-ther and I love to squirm.

Gm **Dm** **Gm** **Dm** **F** **C** **Dm** **A**

I can't hop and I can't fly, But I'll get there by and by.

Dm **F** **A** **Dm**

See___ me twist and see___ me turn As I sli-ther and slide down be-low the green fern.

2. You see me here and you see me there,
Then all of a sudden I just disappear.
I'm down below the earth you know,
Helping little shoots to grow.
All the earth is loosened there
'Cos my tunnels are bringing the rain and the air.

Jean Gilbert

PHOTOCOPIABLE RESOURCES

THE CENTIPEDE

The cen - ti - pede has legs to spare, It real - ly does - n't seem quite fair, When

I have two, but I need some more, then in foot - ball I'd be sure to score.

Sue Nicholls

THE BOOGIE BUGS

1. Clap your hands for the Boo - gie Bugs, Boo - gy - ing a - long un - der - ground.

Clap your hands for the Boo - gie Bugs, Boo - gy - ing a - round and a - round.

Boo - gie to the left, Boo - gie to the right, Boo - gy - ing with - out a sound.

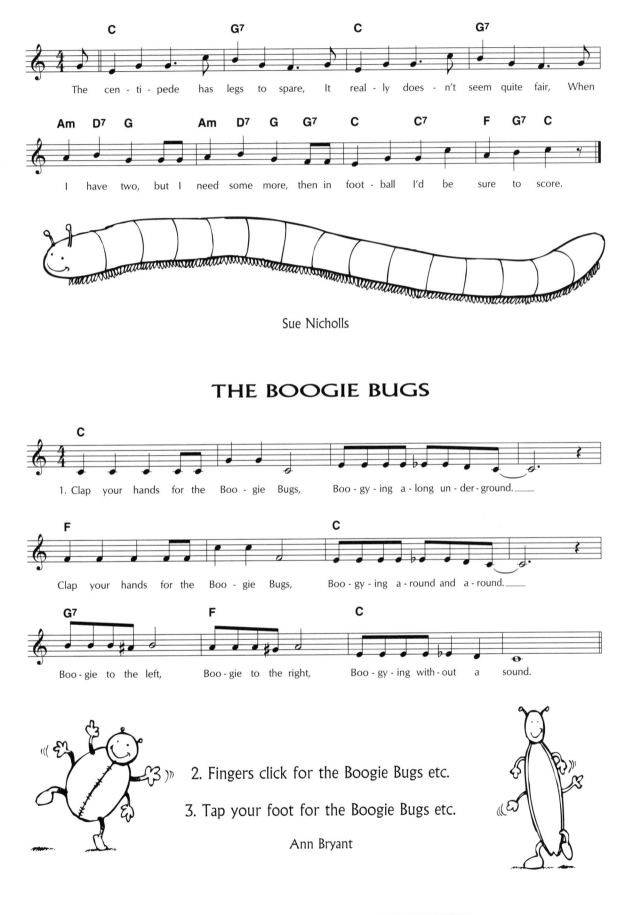

2. Fingers click for the Boogie Bugs etc.

3. Tap your foot for the Boogie Bugs etc.

Ann Bryant

PHOTOCOPIABLE RESOURCES

FLY

(V.2)

1. You see that fly,_____ and now it's gone. Will it fly a - way or set - tle?_____

See it ho - ver in the air, It will land just an - y - where, On cake or cup or ket - tle._____

2. It's up again, in crazy flight,
Now it's crawling on the ceiling.
How can it stay so long up there
Upside down without a care?
Whatever is it feeling?

3. With claws and pads on both my feet,
And with wings to help me fly,
If I could perform like that
I would be an acrobat
With somersaults sky-high!

Jean Gilbert

SNAIL'S PACE

Slow, measured pace

Mov - ing slow - ly, leaves a sil - ver trail, Shell of curls and spi - ral swirls, car - ried by the snail.

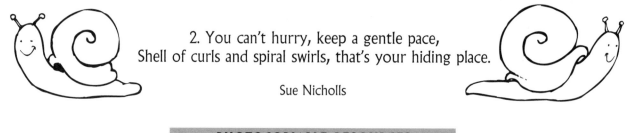

2. You can't hurry, keep a gentle pace,
Shell of curls and spiral swirls, that's your hiding place.

Sue Nicholls

SPIDERS

1. There's a spi - der on the path in - to my gar - den, I can see it scur - ry there, black and cov - ered all with hair. There's a spi - der on the path in - to my gar - den and I hope it turns and runs the oth - er way

2. There's a spider in the corner of the garage
   I can see its web so fine
   Every softly woven line.
   There's a spider in the corner of the garage
   And I hope he's already had a meal.

3. There's a spider on the ceiling of my bedroom
   I can see him up there now
   Clinging on, I don't know how.
   There's a spider on the ceiling of my bedroom
   And I hope he's gone before I go to sleep.

Hazel Hobbs

THEMES
for early years

Draw the dots

◆ Draw five more ladybirds.

◆ Throw a dice and colour in the number of dots which you throw on a ladybird.

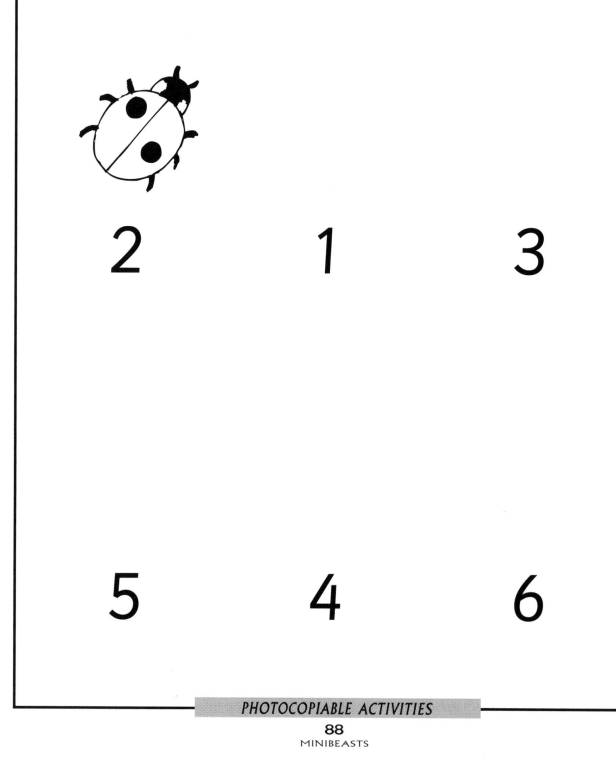

2   1   3

5   4   6

THEMES
for early years

Name _____

Fast and slow

◆ Make sets of fast and slow animals.

THEMES
for early years

Name _____

Worm puppets

◆ Cut out the worm shapes and colour them in.
◆ Cut the slits and put your fingers through the slits to make a puppet.

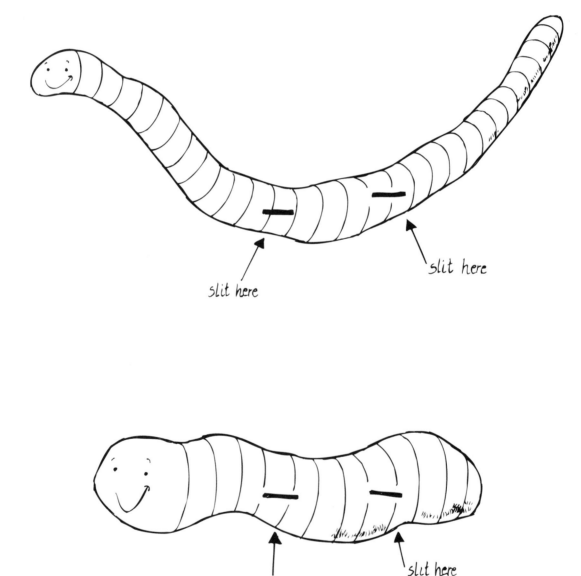

slit here

slit here

slit here

slit here

Wormery maze

◆ Help the worms find their way home.

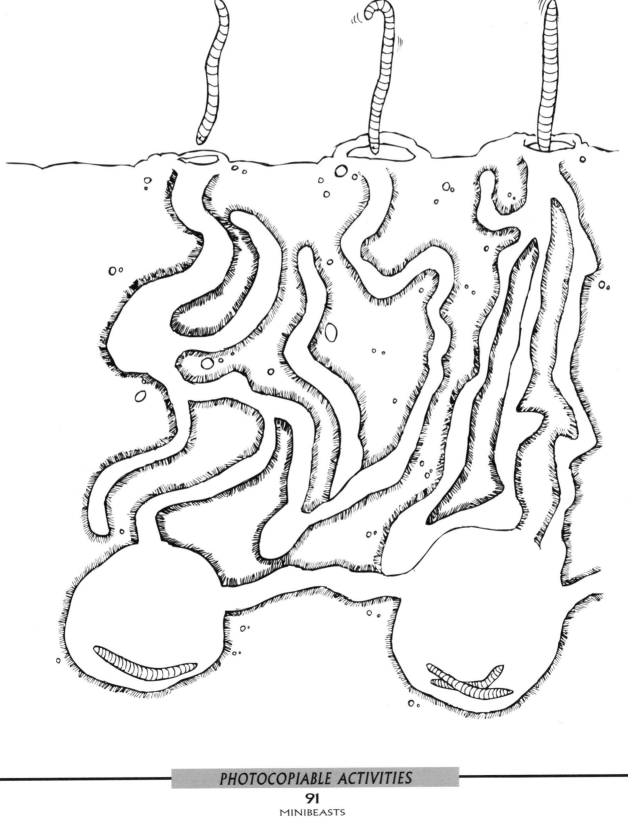

Name _____

Butterfly growth

◆ Put the pictures in the right order to show the changes in the life of a butterfly.

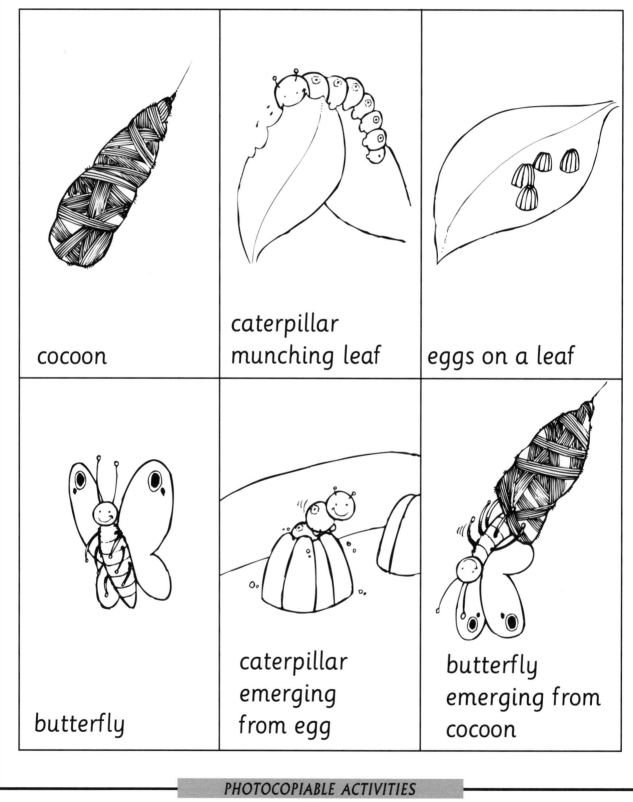

cocoon

caterpillar
munching leaf

eggs on a leaf

butterfly

caterpillar
emerging
from egg

butterfly
emerging from
cocoon

THEMES
for early years

Name _____

Beautiful butterflies

◆ Colour in the butterflies and caterpillars.
Now count how many you can find.

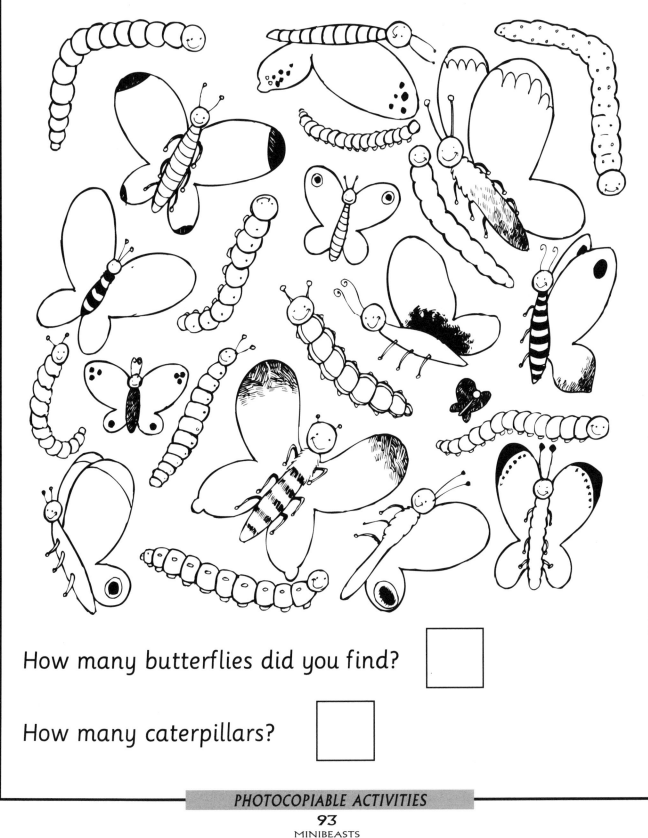

How many butterflies did you find?

How many caterpillars?

THEMES
for early years

Minibeast word search

Can you find these minibeasts hidden in the grid?

(ladybird   spider   worm   fly   snail   bee   beetle)

c	a	v	p	w	o	r	m
s	n	a	i	l	k	h	z
w	t	y	s	f	b	e	e
b	d	b	e	e	t	l	e
s	p	i	d	e	r	o	j
k	w	t	f	u	s	h	e
a	l	m	l	r	o	i	b
l	a	d	y	b	i	r	d

◆ Circle each word when you find it.

How well did you do?

THEMES
for early years

Name _____

Where we found minibeasts

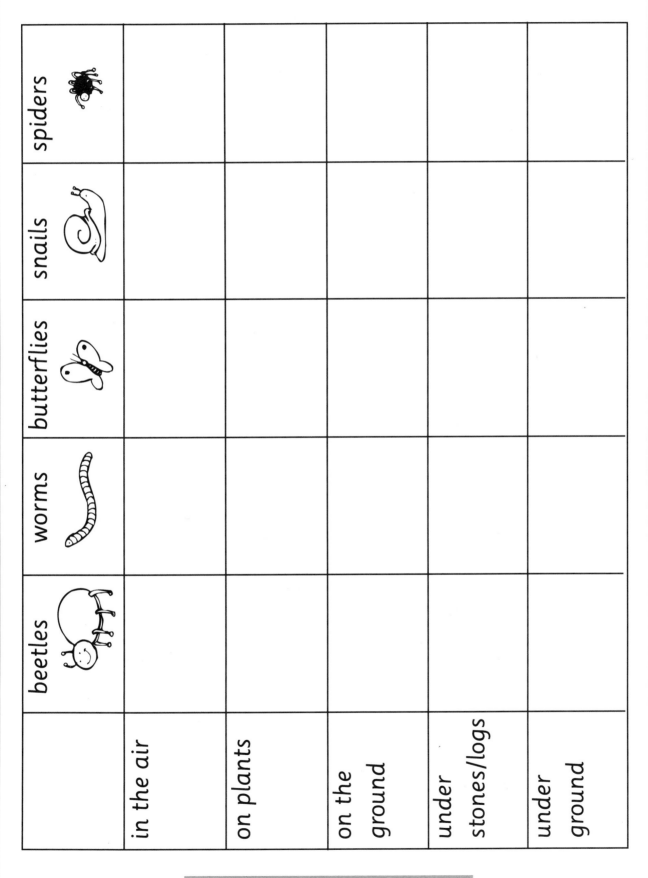

	spiders	snails	butterflies	worms	beetles
in the air					
on plants					
on the ground					
under stones/logs					
under ground					

RECOMMENDED RESOURCES

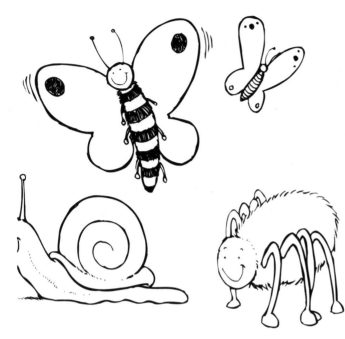

PICTURE AND STORY BOOKS

The Very Hungry Caterpillar by Eric Carle
(Hamish Hamilton)
The Bad Tempered Ladybird by Eric Carle
(Picture Puffin)
It's Too Frightening for Me by Shirley Hughes
(Young Puffin)
Charlotte's Web by EB White (Penguin)
Anansi and the magic yams by Joanna
Troughton (Blackie)
How Anansi captured Tigers stories by Jennifer
Bent (Dutton)
Fancy That by Jan Pienkowski (Orchard Books)
West Indian Folk Tales retold by Philip Sherlock
(Oxford University Press)

INFORMATION BOOKS

Stopwatch Books *Bumble Bee, Butterfly and
Catterpillar, Ladybird, Snail* (A&C Black)
Little Learners series *Lift-the-Flap Bugs and Slugs*
(Usborne)
The Big Bug Search (Usborne)
Rainbows series *The Caterpillar Story* (Evans)

POEMS

'The Spider and the Fly' in *Oxford Treasury of
Children's Poems* ed. (OUP)
Minibeasties selected by Michael Rosen
(Wayland)
Big Billy Peter Dixon (Peter Dixon Books)

POSTERS AND OTHER RESOURCES

Send for *Small Creatures* (A11) a pictures and
poems set comprising photographs and poems
by well-known authors on A4 cards, suitable for
displays or individual work from: Philip Green
Educational. Creatures covered include:
butterflies, ladybirds, snails, spiders and worms.
Pond Life and Small Creatures (P31) is a set of
topic pictures, 12 A4 colour photographs with
teachers' notes also available from: Philip Green
Educational Ltd, 112a Alcester Road, Studley,
Warwickshire B80 7NR.
Insect Lore, Europe, Unit 6 Linford Forum,
Linford Wood, Milton Keynes MK14 6LY
produce a catalogue of resources useful for
insect study, ideal for work with children under
10 years. Includes kits, finger puppets, puzzles
and games.
Heron, Carrwood House, Carrwood Road,
Chesterfield S41 9QB supply science equipment
such as microscopes, magnifiers and specimen
collection packs.
NES Arnold, Early years equipment is arranged
according to the Desirable Outcomes and
comprises equipment, games and puzzles. From:
NES Arnold, Ludlow Hill Road, West Bridgeford,
Nottingham NG2 6HD.
Step-by-Step Ltd, Lavenham Road, Beeches
Trading Estate, Yate, Bristol BS17 5QX produce
craft materials and equipment such as large
magnifying sets.
Asco Educational Supplies, 19 Lockwood Way,
Parkside Lane, Leeds LS11 5TH have mini puzzles,
symmetry sets and games featuring ladybirds and
butterflies.